NO GREATER LOVE

NO GREATER LOVE

The Gripping Story of
Nurse Clara Maass

Written by Mildred Tengbom

Publishing House
St. Louis

Concordia Publishing House, St. Louis, Missouri
Copyright © 1978 Concordia Publishing House

MANUFACTURED IN THE UNITED STATES OF AMERICA

Photos and documents used by permission of The Clara Maass Memorial Hospital, Belleville, New Jersey; RN Magazine, New Jersey; National Archives, Washington, D.C.

Library of Congress Cataloging in Publication Data

Tengbom, Mildred.
    No greater love.

    (Christian heroes)
    Bibliography: p.
    1. Maass, Clara Louise, 1876-1901—Juvenile literature. 2. Nurses—United States—Biography—Juvenile literature. 3. Lutherans—United States—Biography—Juvenile literature. 4. Yellow fever—History—Juvenile literature. I. Title
II. Series
RT37.M17T46   610.73'092'4 (B)   77-28588
ISBN 0-570-07878-4
ISBN 0-570-07883-0 pbk.

To Becky,
my former colleague,
who gave a lifetime in loving nursing service to the
peoples of Nepal

The courage of man is one thing, but that of a maid is more.
  For blood is blood and death is death and grim is the
    battle fore.
And the rose that blooms, tho' blistered by the sleet of an
    open sky,
  Is fairer far than its sisters who sleep in the hothouse
    nigh.

Contents

Acknowledgments

I am debtor to many who helped me in my research for this book. My heartfelt thanks to the librarians at the California School of Nursing at the California Hospital Medical Center, the University of Southern California, and the Anaheim Public Library. Maureen Bartollotta of the Anaheim Public Library deserves special recognition; she worked tirelessly in locating and procuring for me copies of reports and speeches of primary figures in the yellow fever experiments.

I am deeply grateful also to Mrs. Elsie deCordova, only living sister of Clara, who welcomed an interview, and to Pastor Alton N. Allbeck of Riverside, Calif., who conducted the interview on my behalf.

Mr. Albin H. Oberg, president, and Mr. Harold Widman, vice-president, Labor/Public Relations, and staff members ox Clara Maass Memorial Hospital, Mr. Howard B. Hurley of RN Magazine, and members of the Army Nurses Corps kindly read the manuscript and made helpful suggestions. Mr. Jonathan Heller searched for pictures for me at the National Archives. My thanks to these friends, as well as the editors at Concordia Publishing House and especially Patricia C. McKissack.

My thanks, as always, also to my family and friends who constantly encourage me.■

8

Author's Note

In preparing this manuscript I relied heavily on books that gave information as to the life and times of Clara Maass. My research led me into a study of the nursing methods of the 1900s, the Spanish-American War and the mood of that day, and the long history of the havoc yellow fever wrought and the struggle to overcome it. Especially in connection with the latter subject I discovered varying reports. Whenever possible I tried to go back to primary sources. I tried also to view the yellow fever experiments through the eyes of those working most closely with the experiments: Dr. Gorgas, Dr. Guiteras, General Wood, Dr. Agramonte, and Dr. Carroll. The accounts of each of these men had something a little different to offer.

In regard to the purpose of the experiments in which Clara was involved, I have felt that most accounts have not been clear. Sometimes it has been stated only in a general way: "in connection with yellow fever." As I compared the various accounts, I finally arrived at the viewpoint I present in this book.

I should mention also that the conversation in the book, in most cases, though not all, is, of course, fictional, but the facts presented in the conversations have been researched.

We do not know for certain that Clara was present at the Thanksgiving celebration of the German Hospital, but in any event the celebration was of such significance that she most surely would have read and heard about it.

The scene where Clara is introduced to the men of the Yellow Fever Commission is fictionalized, as we do not know exactly when she met them, although she worked closely with them. The writer used this scene as a writer's technique to introduce these characters to her readers.

In regard to Dr. Gorgas, the scene in the Episcopal church in Havana is fictionalized, although we know that Dr. Gorgas often assisted at or conducted services. The section on parabolani I have inserted because I felt, after reading extensively about Dr. Gorgas, that it best reflected the life and spirit of the man. The other words, however, in that scene are Dr. Gorgas' own words.

I myself was profoundly stirred as I worked on the book. Clara's courage and sacrifice of love moved me deeply. Memories flooded back to me also.

I remembered being inoculated twice for yellow fever and being asked if I was allergic to eggs, because the vaccine was produced in eggs.

Like Clara, my own mother was a "mother's helper" when she was a child, and she often related to me what it had been like.

As a shy farm girl who had to go to the big city for further education, I could identify with Clara's feelings as she approached Nurse Steeber to enroll as a student nurse.

From earliest childhood I, too, have been captured by the desire Clara cherished, to live a life that will have significance.

Clara traveled on troop ships of the 1900s. I traveled to India in 1945 on an American troop transport and an Indian troop transport and spent 10 days in an Italian prisoner-of-war camp in

10

Ismailia, Egypt, where I was smitten with amoebic dysentery, one of the maladies Clara nursed in her patients.

The tropics hold the same fascination for me as they did for Clara and Dr. Gorgas.

I, too, had an encounter with dengue fever and know what it feels like to have the "bones breaking."

My colleague, Becky Grimsrud, to whom this book is dedicated, nursed typhoid fever patients in India, and, as I was at her side, I witnessed what tropical fevers can do to a human being.

I also could identify with Clara's desire to spend her life in service among people where the need is very great. I had seven gloriously happy years among the Nepalese in India and eight and one-half years on the lower slopes of Kilimanjaro in East Africa with my family.

I know, too, that one finds overseas, working in out-of-the-way places and, in many cases, under primitive conditions, some of the world's most highly educated, brilliant, and compassionate people that our generation has produced. Clara experienced this also as she became acquainted with Major Gorgas, Dr. Guiteras, Dr. Lazear, Dr. Carroll, and Dr. Agramonte and heard about General Wood and Major Reed.

It is the prayer of my heart that at least some who read this book will be inspired to become parabolani, gamblers who pour out their lives for others. The world needs them today more than ever.

Mildred Tengbom

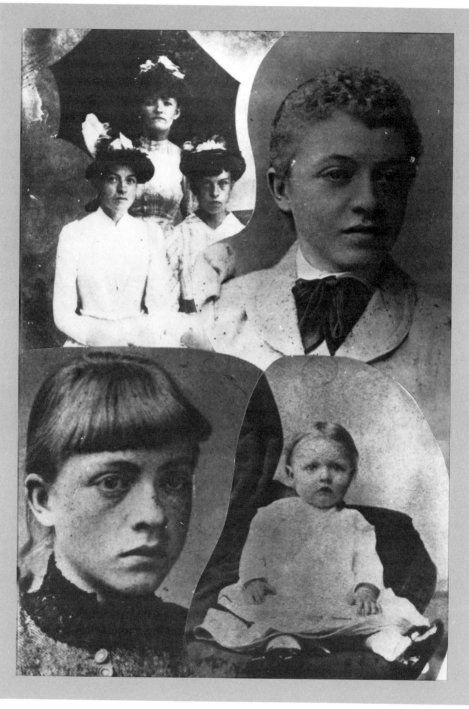

BOTTOM RIGHT: Clara Maass at age 18 months; BOTTOM LEFT: Clara Maass at age 14; TOP RIGHT: Clara Maass at age 16; TOP LEFT: Clara Maass (left sitting) and sisters.

1

Good-bye, Home!

Gerrman immigrant to Livingston, New Jersey, tall, spare Robert Maass threw a rope over the load of furniture stacked helter-skelter on top of the hay rack. On the other side Hedwig Maass, his neatly dressed wife, stretched up on tiptoe to grab the rope, pulled it taut, wound it around a post, and then tossed it back to her husband.

"We'll have to be sure the rocking chair is secure," she called.

"Are the children ready to leave?" Slight irritation and a sense of being uptight colored Robert Maass' tone.

"Cla-a-ra!" Hedwig Maass' clear voice hung in the morning air. "Have you gathered the children together?"

"I'll get them, Mama." Twelve-year old Clara tossed her honey-brown braids over her shoulder. She raced off in pursuit of baby Harriet, whose black sateen bloomer bottom was disappearing inside the house.

Clack, clack, clack, Clara's high-buttoned black shoes echoed in the hallway of the empty house stripped now of the cane matting that usually lay on the floor. Clara squinted into the parlor. No baby. She heard a snicker. Clara opened the front closet door. No baby. She walked down the hall and peered into what had been her papa's and mama's bedroom. There sat Harriet on the floor, trying to pull off one of her shoes.

The room still smelled of her father's pipe, even though the scatter rugs from the floor and the lace curtains from the windows were gone.

Clara reached down to gather the baby in her arms. She buried her face in the silky hair of her little sister.

"We're going to leave," she whispered. "I don't want to leave. It's been so much fun being able to stay home. I love the farm. And I love being with you. I don't know why, but I just like being with my family."

A tear trickled down her cheek. She brushed it dry in her sister's hair.

"There, there," she said, "things will work out. Somehow I'll be able to do all the things I've dreamed about doing. Some day I'll become somebody and be able to do something worthwhile."

"Cla-a-ra!" She heard her mother call again.

"Coming, Mama!"

Papa was standing in the front part of the hay rack, holding the reins of the dapple-gray horses that would pull the load of furniture. A neighbor already had bought the team and the wagon. Papa would return it to him after they had unloaded their furniture. Mama would drive the horses for their big black market wagon.

Margareta and Emma scrambled up to sit on the front bench with their mother. Robert and Sophie crawled up into the back. They shoved over the woven straw lunch hamper and the oak carved cabinet clock, safely wrapped in a quilt, and settled down on the floor of the buggy. Next to them was the clothes basket with the dishes wrapped in towels, and the box with the kerosene lamps with overalls pushed in around to keep the lamps from breaking.

Clara lifted up the baby and put her into Sophie's arms. Then

14

Clara herself climbed in and squeezed into the only space left. She reached over the took the baby from Sophie.

"Ready?" Clara's mother had been looking back, watching. Clara flashed a smile. "Ready, Mother."

"Giddap," clucked her mother, flicking the reins.

The big round carriage wheels creaked as the horses strained forward. The Maass family was on their way to live again in the city.

The horses' hooves, going clop, clop, clop on the dirt road kicked up little puffs of dust. No sunshade shielded those in the back of the wagon. Clara felt the sun warm on her head.

"Your hair's red in the sun," Bob observed.

"It isn't!" Clara retorted. She shooed away the flies from baby Harriet's face.

Clop-clop, clop-clop. The carriage rolled onto a wooden bridge that spanned a brook merrily chasing its way through the meadow.

"Good-bye, brook!" Clara called softly, then in her mind she continued, "I won't be able to wade in you anymore, or build dams in the spring." And another tear escaped and matted baby Harriet's soft hair.

Around a bend in the road the wooden Livingston schoolhouse came into sight.

"Good-bye, school!" Clara called, fluttering her eyelids fast.

She began to turn questions over in her mind. "Wonder if we'll live in a dingy old tenement flat again? Wonder where I'll be sent to work this time? I wish we could have stayed on the farm! Wonder how many babies the family for whom I work will have? Wonder if I'll have to get up at 3 a.m. to feed the smallest baby? I liked the farm better than the city. Wonder if I'll get a chance to go to school?" she thought.

As though she understood her daughter's thoughts, her mother reached around the outside of the front seat and let her hand rest briefly on Clara's shoulder.

"Raw leather will stretch," she said simply.

Clara smiled shakily. Mama was trying to tell her, she realized, that she had confidence in her that she would be able to make the necessary adjustments. The thought made Clara feel good. Things will work out, she thought. Some day my dreams to be someone and do something worthwhile will come true.

"Good-bye, farm home!" Clara called out, only the words were locked up inside herself. "Good-bye, home!" She blinked fast and then began to play with her baby sister.■

2

The Day That Changed Clara's Life

Back in Orange, New Jersey, Robert Maass got a job in a hat factory. But the work was seasonable, and the pay was poor. Every few years another crying baby announced its arrival at the home of Robert and Hedwig. Then there was another mouth to feed, another body to clothe. Too many mouths to feed. Too many bodies to clothe. There was no alternative. The oldest child of their family must learn to provide for herself.

So Clara did as she had done before. She hired out to be a "mother's helper." That involved all kinds of work, from scrubbing floors to tending babies, to carrying in wood, to building a fire, to weeding gardens, to rubbing clothes by hand on a washboard, to mending clothes, to running errands to the store. Gratitude that the family she worked for allowed time for her to go to high school lightened the load. Home from school by four o'clock, she mechanically did her household chores, while her inquisitive mind turned over what she had learned during her day in school. And her dream never left her—her dream to one day be someone and do something worthwhile.

The years passed by as though they were bogged down in chewing gum. At last it was 1891 and Clara was 15.

"The Newark Orphan Asylum's looking for a housekeeper," she overheard one day when she was in the General Store.

"How much do they pay?" she timidly asked.

The proprietor peered over his black-rimmed glasses. "Why? Are you interested, Miss? Seems to me I heard $10 a month. But then I 'spect you get your board and bed too."

Clara pondered the opportunity. So what if she had to work seven days a week, as the store proprietor said? Ten dollars was $10. With $10 she would be able to send her mother $5 and still have $5 for herself. "Well, I could at least go over and talk to them," she thought. And then, chuckling to herself, "I hope my shaky knees will hold me up."

So she went. The matron must have liked what she heard and saw. When Clara walked out the door of the orphanage, the job was hers.

Picking up after, cleaning, cooking, and doing the laundry for a whole household of sometimes obstreperous orphans was even more difficult than being a mother's helper, Clara discovered. At times she despaired and cried silently into her pillow at night. Her face lost its little-girl look. Sad eyes peered out from under heavy lids. But determination to make the best of things reflected itself in careful attention to grooming. And awareness that she was developing into a young woman revealed itself in curled hair.

Then came the crisp Thanksgiving Day, Nov. 30, 1893, which changed the entire course of Clara's life. The imposing, solid, three-story with basement, red-brick German hospital in the Germantown section of Newark was celebrating. The 23-year-old hospital was dedicating Trefz Hall, properly called "The Training School for Nurses."

At the gala celebration at Caledonia Park, to which people from the entire city came, the call went out to girls between the

18

ages of 20 and 40 to apply for training.

"They should be of good character and with proof of physical strength and ability," the speaker explained. "They should have completed at least a general school education and have a fair knowledge of English."

The call reached 17-year-old Clara Louise Maass, who had managed to get the day off and was at the park. The fact that she was three years too young didn't deter her. She long had dreamed of investing her life in something worthwhile. Two years in the orphanage had given her valuable experience. But it was time to move, she decided. Here was her opportunity.

The day she planned to present herself at the hospital, she dressed with care. She washed and brushed smooth her soft light-brown hair, pulling it back severely and coiling it into a bun at the back. She curled the bangs in front to soften the lines around her face. She polished her black kid shoes, and then, pulling them on over her long black cotton stockings, she buttoned the 10 buttons on the side of each shoe with a buttonhook.

She slipped on her black woolen skirt, lined with crisp percaline and interlined with crinoline. The three-and-one-quarter-yard sweep at the bottom made her slight frame seem fuller. She chose a plain, long-sleeved, white blouse, considering it more appropriate than a short-sleeved, low-necked, frilly one. She also hoped the plain one would add years to her.

With long hat pins she pinned on her one black felt hat, resplendent with light blue taffetine rosettes, three feather quills, and a large gilt buckle. A wide blue velvet ribbon encircled the base of the crown. She made sure she had a fresh, linen handkerchief. Next she threw over her shoulders the woolen melton cape she had saved money to buy, with its lining of black sateen and its high-standing collar trimmed with brown bear fur. The hundred-inch sweep of the cape at its bottom also gave fullness to her spare figure. Over her shoes she pulled black cloth overshoes and fastened the buckles. Finally, slipping on her gloves and buttoning them, she stepped out into the crisp winter day.

The snow crunched under her feet as she walked to the corner where the trolley that would take her across town stopped for passengers. As she waited, it began to snow, the flakes drifting down softly and silently.

Once on the trolley, she began to wonder whatever had prompted her to do what she was doing. She leaned her head against the glass of the window and stared out at the falling snow. Up, up, up the hill the trolley climbed, its iron wheels screeching on the frosty rails.

On the corner of Newton and West Bank she alighted. After the trolley clanked off, she stood for a moment gazing at the city spread below her, its church steeples and smokestacks from its industries knifing the sky. Then she took a long look at Trefz Hall, its freshly painted exterior shining all the more because of the snowy carpet all around it. It was a huge house, three stories with basement, gabled, its walls of white wood siding with green shutters framing the windows. A decorative front veranda supported on two ends by three tall colonnades grouped together and boasting an elaborately carved low railing, graced the front of the house. The house, Clara decided, was elegant indeed. She had heard that inside were not only bathrooms and 14 bedrooms but also a lecture room and a parlor.

Her eyes shifted to the imposing red-brick hospital. Then, without further hesitation, she walked quickly towards it. At the bottom of the stairs she paused briefly, drew a deep breath, and began to climb the dozen steps that led to the front door. At the top she stamped her feet, pulled off her boots, shook herself to dislodge the snow, and then pushed open the massive wooden door. She stepped inside and found herself in an entrance 10 feet wide with walls 15 feet high. She moved forward timidly, then noticed a reception room to one side.

"I would like to see Head Nurse Anna Seeber," she heard her voice saying to the buxom volunteer from the Frauenverein, the Women's Guild, who was seated behind the desk.

"Be seated," invited the woman, as she arose to go and deliver the message to Miss Seeber.

The rustling of crinoline skirts announced the return of the

20

volunteer, but not the volunteer only. To Clara's surprise, Miss Steeber had come in person to receive her.

Even in her astonishment Clara's eyes did not miss the crisp blue-and-white-striped uniform Anna Steeber was wearing. It dropped to within two inches of the floor. Over it she wore a bibless, starched white apron, the band of which nipped in her waist. A white muslin cap, pleated around the edge and with a black ribbon running around the crown, perched on her smooth brown hair, which was drawn back severely into coils piled on top of her head. A thermometer was pushed through a buttonhole of her bodice.

Nurse Steeber extended a water-wrinkled hand. Clara took it, then curtsied briefly.

"Yes?" Miss Steeber inquired. "You wanted to see me?"

"I'd . . . I'd like to enroll to become a nurse."

Anna Steeber studied Clara carefully.

"You're young," she said in her stolid way. "We usually don't take girls until they are 20. Some training schools don't admit them until they are 25." She gave a mirthless little laugh and added, "In fact, some say only the middle-aged should apply and those who have been tamed by marriage and the troubles of raising many children.

"I am young," Clara admitted, "but I also have raised many children even though I have not married yet. Since I was 9 or 10 years old I have worked as a mother's helper in a number of homes. At present I take care of children seven days a week at the Newark Orphanage."

"So," said Anna Steeber.

Clara had pulled off her gloves and stood twisting them. Nurse Steeber's eyes dropped to Clara's reddened, chapped hands. "If you are not afraid of work, perhaps you will do. It has been said of nurses," she added wryly, "that those who look the most worn out, and those who give tirelessly of themselves for others, never thinking of themselves, they are the best nurses."

Anna Steeber's blue eyes took in the girl's simple but well-pressed clothes, her spare frame, her hair pulled back tightly into a knot. Serious blue eyes looked out from behind fragile gold frames.

"Come with me to my office," she said at length. "We will talk further."

Clara followed her down the hall, peeking into the examining rooms, the bathrooms, and an apothecary shop as she went. Through an open door she caught a glimpse of a ward with beds in neat rows. At the end of the hall they came to a stairway.

"My office is on the second floor," Nurse Steeber explained.

Clara's eyes lit up as they entered Nurse Steeber's attractive, homelike office. White-painted woodwork and doors. Wallpaper on the walls. A couch with a brightly colored knit afghan tossed over it. Some small square tables, covered with starched, white cloths, edged with stiff crocheted lace. Plants and gas table lamps with colored glass shades sat on the tables. A brilliant flowering poinsettia brightened the room. Straight-backed wooden chairs, with attractive carving, and a rocking chair invited visitors to sit. Pictures, tilted downwards, as though to examine those sitting below them, hung on the walls. A queer-looking brown box on the wall caught Clara's attention. She squinted, then decided it probably was a telephone. "Wonder if they'll teach me how to use it," she thought. Then her eyes noticed the magazines and books in the room. She drew her eyebrows together, trying to read the titles. "I could be thoroughly happy if I had all the time in the world to read," she thought.

Nurse Steeber motioned Clara to a chair. Then she went over to the iron potbellied stove that stood in one corner, opened the door, and threw in a shovelful of coal. Coming back, she sat down across from Clara and studied again the small face and the serious blue eyes.

"You know German, of course?"

"And English too."

"You'll need German more. This is a German hospital. All the lectures will be in German and some in Latin."

"I had two years of Latin in high school."

Surprise. "Good. . . . Nursing is not an easy career, you

understand. Here at the German Hospital doctors understand the need for trained nurses, but after you leave here, you may find it different elsewhere. Some doctors say," and Miss Steeber's nose twitched ever so slightly, "that nurses are in much the same position as housemaids and need little teaching beyond poultice-making and the enforcement of cleanliness and attention to the patient's wants. Others say that a nurse is a confidential servant, but still only a servant."

Clara's chin quivered. She pressed her lips together. Nurse Steeber looked closely at her and then continued. "Florence Nightingale said, and rightly so, that instructors cannot put into students what is not already there. Our aim is to bring out whatever abilities you have. Training is enabling you to use and develop the ability you already possess."

Clara's heart lurched with joy. "Why, that's what I want!" she thought. "I know I can do much more than I have been doing."

Nurse Steeber walked over to the stove, picked up a stoker, opened the door, and vigorously shook up the coals. The fire blazed into life. She shut the door, hung up the stoker, and sat down again.

"The doctors here are very demanding," she continued, dropping her voice. "Before we opened our own training school we had Red Cross nurses working here. But they were as proud of their profession as our doctors are of theirs. The doctors and the nurses tangled so often that finally all the nurses resigned and walked out." She picked a thread off the cloth on the table. "It isn't going much better with our first-year class either. I don't know how many will finish the course."

She smoothed her already smooth apron. "You are aware, of course, that nurses are not regarded highly enough yet to be paid well. You probably will receive less than a laundress." She shot another inquiring look at Clara.

Clara didn't have any idea how much a laundress received. "It surely must be more than the $10 I've been getting at the orphanage," she thought.

"If, after you graduate," Nurse Steeber said, "you do private

23

duty, you'll work at least 56 hours weekly and probably more. When you nurse a patient in a home, you must be prepared to respond day and night. Your salary probably will be $15 a week."

Fifteen dollars a <u>week.</u> Clara gasped. "I'll be rich," she thought. "I'll be able to send Mama much money to help her with the family."

"Private duty nurses," Anna Steeber went on, "nurse patients recovering from the fevers: typhoid, typhus, and the most dreaded of all, when it appears now and again, yellow fever. Tuberculosis is perhaps our greatest enemy. And pneumonia. Some nurses become obstetrical nurses. If you go on an obstetrical case, you must be prepared to stay from one to three months. Some families become so fond of their obstetrical nurses they keep them on permanently as live-in nurses. But perhaps"—Anna Steeber reached over to snip off some dead leaves from the plant at her side—"you will stay on at the hospital. We need graduate nurses to train the probationers. Of if you are really adventuresome, you might even find yourself caring for wounded soldiers in Cuba. With all the stories in the papers these days about the atrocities and inhumane acts of the Spanish in Cuba, a lot of feeling is getting stirred up. Some are suggesting we owe it to the people of Cuba to help them shake off their shackles from Spain. If that should happen, and our country went to war, there most surely will be a call for nurses. After all the fuss Florence Nightingale has been stirring up for properly organized and equipped military hospitals so the wounded and ill can be cared for adequately, no nation is going to go to war without making plans for medical aid."

Anna Steeber paused. It had been a long speech for her. Her last remarks had triggered Clara's imagination. Clara saw herself boarding a military transport. Clara saw herself bending over a wounded soldier on the battlefield. Clara saw herself walking with a kerosene lantern up and down the rows in a tent hospital. She stared unseeing past Miss Steeber. As though she knew what Clara was thinking, Nurse Steeber's next blunt remarks hauled Clara back to the German hospital.

"Oh, I know it sounds glamorous. But in truth, most of the time nursing is just a lot of grueling, hard work. Hospitals take advantage of nurses." She dropped her voice again. A tinge of bitterness crept in. "I suspect that is why the numbers of training schools for nurses have grown as they have. Just eight years ago, in 1890, there were only 35 schools with 471 graduate nurses. I've heard it predicted that by the time you graduate, or shall we say by 1900, that we'll have over 400 schools and at least 3,500 nurses."

Anna Steeber straightened the books and magazines on the table.

"Of course," she continued, "we must remember many of these schools are private and the standards vary greatly. Many do not begin to measure up to the training offered by the University of Maryland Hospital in Baltimore, the Connecticut Training School at New Haven, the Bellevue Hospital in New York, the Massachusetts General Hospital, the Montreal General Hospital, or the Illinois Training School in Chicago."

Miss Steeber sat a little straighter as though she was proud to have been able to have intoned such a long list of impressive-sounding names.

"Here at the German hospital," she drew herself even more erect, "your training will be thorough. Our 14 German doctors will see to that.

"We're proud of our directors too. They are progressive. They got rid of the chicken coops, which were sources of so much infection. We have telephones," motioning to the one hanging on her wall, "and steam laundry machines for washing and ironing. I even hear talk of installing elevators in a couple of years. We also have private rooms now, equal to those you find in the finest hospitals. And separate entrances so we can admit patients with communicable diseases like diphtheria, without danger of infecting the other patients."

"As a student nurse, will I receive any pay?" Clara asked hesitantly, yet feeling she must have an answer.

"Oh, did I neglect to give you that information? You will receive your board and room and $5 a month spending money."

Clara gulped. "I wonder if Mama can get along with less for a couple of years," she worried. "What is the nature of the training?" she asked.

"Your first year will be spent in the classroom and in the wards. The second year we shall send you as a private nurse to homes to gain further experience. The salary you earn during that year, of course will be handed over to the hospital, as you are considered to be in training. But if you are successful in graduating, you will receive $100 bonus at graduation."

Relief replaced anxiety. She did some quick calculation. "That will almost make up the difference for Mama," she consoled herself.

A few questions followed. Was Clara willing to place herself unquestioningly under the authority of the head nurse for the next two years? Was she willing to work hard without complaining, to follow doctors' orders, to learn to observe patients carefully, to keep their confidences, to administer drugs with utmost caution? Did she consider herself able to work under imperious and often difficult-to-get-along-with doctors?

Clara answered affirmatively, feeling her stomach knot with each answer.

Anna Steeber had no more questions to ask. She stood up. The pale, feeble rays of the winter sun slanted into the room. A sudden gust of wind outside rattled the shutters and with a sharp crack broke off one of the long icicles hanging down in front of the window.

Nurse Steeber walked over to the door. Clara followed her. Miss Steeber opened the door and stood aside to let Clara pass through it.

Clara was having difficulty pulling on her gloves. The palms of her hands were moist and the gloves stuck. She felt Miss Steeber's eyes on her. Her confusion grew. "Is she not going to tell me whether or not I am admitted?" she worried. "I'll bet I didn't make it."

Miss Steeber relaxed her stiff mouth long enough to crack out a whisper of a smile. "Arrange with the orphanage to leave as soon as you can," she said. "As soon as you move in, we shall begin to train you." ■

26

3

K. P. Duty, Carbolic Acid,
and Student Griping

To begin with, after moving into Trefz Hall, Clara kept wondering if she would wake up and discover it was all a dream. After years of sweating it out as someone else's hired girl, here she was, able to call this elegant place home and able to get professional training.

The parlor especially of Trefz Hall had class, Clara thought, with the delicate ecru-colored lace curtains at the windows, the richly colored red and gold oriental rug on the waxed hardwood floor, the black grand piano, supported on massive legs, the pump organ, and the red velvet sofas, stuffed with horse hair and made comfortable with springs. A huge Bible with board-stiff embossed covers lay on a richly carved and highly polished square table in the center of the room. Overlooking all was the full-bosomed, life-sized Mrs. Christina Trefz, immobile in a portrait and enclosed in an ornate gold picture frame that rested on a large easel. Mrs. Trefz had given Trefz Hall to the hospital.

The only problem was, Clara said to herself, that she had practically no time to spend in the handsome room. Shifts were either from 7 a.m. to 7 p.m. or 7 p.m. to 7 a.m. Lectures were squeezed in between. One afternoon a week the student nurses were granted some time off, and four hours on Sunday, but that was all. Lights went out at 10 p.m. every night. There was no point in a weary nurse trying to feign sickness in order to get some much-needed rest, for a sick nurse either had to forfeit her pay or make up her time.

The first year of Clara's training, three other girls shared Trefz Hall with her the entire time: Sophie Bruckner, Sarah Filer, and Madeline Gill. Carrie Frank and six other girls from the first-year class were in and out between assignments for private duty nursing. As the year progressed, however, one by one the second-year students quit. In the end only Carrie Frank was left.

"It's the everlasting cleaning that gets to me," one of the girls complained one day. The girls were in the kitchen preparing special dishes for some of the patients. "We have Florence Nightingale to thank for all this emphasis on wet dusting. 'The only way I know to remove dust,'" she began to quote, almost sarcastically, from Florence Nightingale's Notes on Nursing, "'the plague of all lovers of fresh air, is to wipe everything with a damp cloth. As to floors, the only really clean floor I know is the lackered floor, which is wet rubbed and dry rubbed every morning to remove the dust.'"

Sophie was browning meat. After stewing it she would squeeze the juice from it for broth. Now, as she stirred it, tantalizing odors crept out of the pan.

Sophie chuckled. "Florence even thought the outside walls of the house should be tiled so fire departments could circulate in the neighborhoods regularly and hose them down."

"I wish we could hose down the walls in the wards instead of having to scrub them by hand," Clara said. She was standing near the stove.

"Oh, but we have to admit Florence has done a lot for us nurses," one of the girls countered, taking the big wire whisk off its hook and vigorously whipping up some eggs for custard. "Think what it must have been like in hospitals 25 years ago. Imagine nursing without carbolic acid for example." She shuddered.

"Say, I never thought of that before."

"How would you treat the patient in Room 20 without carbolic acid?"

"You mean the one who had his legs crushed by the locomotive?"

"Yes. Or the fellow who was kicked by the horse?"

Clara entered the conversation again. "We can thank Lister for carbolic acid," she said. She was standing, her round gold watch in hand, ready to time huge pots of water when they began to boil. "The filthy water we get from the Passaic River!" she interjected. "If only all our people boiled their drinking water we wouldn't have so many fevers. Why can't we prevent illnesses rather than just treat them?" She took off her glasses, lifted the lid, and peered into one of the blue-speckled enamel kettles.

"That's what prompted Lister to conduct his experiments," the first girl said. "He was distressed over all the wounds and injuries that got infected. Then he read how Louis Pasteur, the French chemist, thought microbes caused infection."

Sophie, who was pouring her custard mixture into casseroles interrupted, "And so he began to ask, 'How can we kill the microbes?'"

"And then he read another article," Clara chimed in, "about carbolic acid being dumped on sewage and ridding it of its odor. And he said to himself, 'Bacteria causes odor, carbolic acid kills that odor. Maybe carbolic acid kills bacteria too.'" She peered into the pots again. The water was bubbling furiously. She turned down the gas, looked again to see if the water was maintaining its boil, and then consulted her watch.

"It did too!" the first girl called out triumphantly. "Enter the carbolic age . . . Well, at least we all remember the lecture on Lister, don't we?"

The girls laughed.

"But wouldn't it be exciting to make a discovery like Lister?"

Clara asked. "Find something that would really help people in a big way?"

"Say," one popped up, "what's wrong with the patient in Room 13?"

"Hypochondriac. At least that's what the doctors say."

"What about Room 33?"

"Homesickness, pure, plain, and simple. She came over from Germany a month ago to get married. But I guess she's already discovered her man isn't what she thought he was. She just lies there and cries and cries."

"I expect I'd be homesick too if I went to Germany," one of the girls said sympathetically.

Clara was lifting her kettles off the stove. "I think it would be fun to travel," she said firmly.

The door to the kitchen opened. One of the second-year students who had been on private duty in a home dragged herself in.

"I'm beat," she declared, slumping wearily into a chair. "I've never worked so hard or been so tired before in all my life."

"You're on your way to becoming an exemplary nurse," Sophie said. "In fact, I think I see a halo forming."

"Don't try to be funny." The girl folded her arms on the table, then rested her head on them.

"Here, have something to eat," Clara coaxed. "Some coffee? And some bread? You'll feel better."

"I suppose I shouldn't complain," the girl said. "Has anyone given you girls the lecture on Linda Richards yet?"

"You mean the first graduate nurse in the U. S.?"

The girl nodded. "Last year when I was in training our matron made sure we understood what Miss Richard's days were like." She laughed a short wintry laugh. "The nurses then arose at 5:30 a.m. and left the wards at 9 p.m. Their beds were in little rooms between the wards. Each nurse was responsible for six patients, day and night. Miss Richards said she sometimes got up nine times a night to answer calls. Wonder how many times I was up last night?" She yawned and sat up, putting her elbow on the table and cradling her

30

BOTTOM LEFT: Head Nurse, Ann Seeber who interviewed Clara Maass; BOTTOM RIGHT: German Hospital where Clara Maass was trained as a nurse; CENTER LEFT: Christina Trefz Nursing School parlor; CENTER LEFT: Trefz Hall where Clara Maass lived and worked as a student nurse; TOP: Nurse Clara Mass (standing far right) with fellow nursing graduates.

chin in her upturned palm. "Every other week they got off one afternoon from two to five o'clock. She said the first year she went to church once. And all the bottles were numbered, but not labeled, because they were not supposed to know what medicines they gave." She took a long draught from her coffee cup.

Sophie chuckled. "But what a long way <u>they</u> had come compared to what was going on a hundred years ago."

"I know," Clara interrupted. "I was reading the rules for one of the hospitals back in 1789. 'No dirt, rags, or bones may be thrown from the windows.' Can you imagine what would happen here if we began to throw bones and rags out the windows? Can't you see Nurse Steeber's face?"

They all laughed.

"Or how about the rule that declared that nurses were to change the sheets once in a fortnight," Clara continued, "and the shirts of the patients once in four days, and their drawers and stockings once a week—if found necessary."

"How icky!" exclaimed Sophie, holding her nose.

Clara went on. "The book also emphasized that 'all nurses who disobey orders, get drunk, neglect their patients, quarrel or fight with other nurses, or quarrel with men, shall be immediately discharged.'"

The girls laughed again. Then Clara grew serious. "But we've so much left to learn. Take that typhoid patient in Room 21. For 30 days his temperature has hovered around 102 to 103 degrees. We've lowered him daily in tubs filled with cold water and a 20-pound ice cube. But still the fever persists."

"Typhoid fever is bad," Sophie admitted. "But we can be glad we don't have many yellow fever plagues any more. At least not in this part of the country."

"And glad we have a hospital like this to train in," Clara said, "and doctors who are always searching for answers to problems. Even if sometimes they are bears to work for."

"That's for sure," Sophie said. "But then we have to remember that they often aren't appreciated or understood. You know that German Saengerfest we had last Sunday for the benefit of the hospital?"

The girls nodded. "Wasn't that something?" one of them said. "Those 500 voices in the choir. That was really something."

"Well," Sophie continued, "I went to church Sunday at the Franklin Street Methodist Episcopal Church. The pastor, Rev. James Boyd Brady, was sizzling because of the Song Fest."

"I can't believe it," Clara said. "Who would object to Wagnerian music?"

"Or ballet?"

"It probably was the ballet. Anyway, the Rev. Brady practically consigned all Germans to the pit."

"You're not serious."

"I am! He called the Song Fest a 'great, menacing, living curse.' He said we Germans walk around the streets, sell beer, and gamble as though we owned the whole country and the Constitution. That we march through the streets as though nobody else has a right but we."

The girls chuckled.

"I knew the feeling of the townspeople against us Germans was pretty strong," Clara said, "but I didn't know it was that strong."

"You'll have to admit last Sunday's celebration was pretty overwhelming," Sophie said. "All that red, white, and blue bunting draped on the outside walls of Kresge's, Hahne's, and the other department stores."

"And the trains unloading visitors from all over the country."

"We have to admit that we as Germans are proud," Sophie was trying to be honest. "Even we nurses don't like the arrogance of some of our German doctors."

"That's for sure!" The girls chimed in agreement.

"But we Germans work hard," Clara protested. "We're intelligent, and we get things done. Take our hospital here. I'm proud of it—and justly so, I think."

"Say, did you see the time?" Sophie interrupted. "We better hurry with getting these dishes washed up, or we'll be late to lecture."

And five minutes later the kitchen at Trefz Hall was empty.■

BOTTOM LEFT: Nurse Clara Maass standing; BOTTOM RIGHT: Pastor Lehlbach who helped start the German Hospital; MIDDLE LEFT: The German Hospital in the late 1800's; MIDDLE RIGHT: Dr. Fridolin Ill; TOP: Nurse Clara Maass, Head Nurse at the German Hospital. (background—"A bit of Germantown.")

4

No Time for Bandaging Today

How did a hospital like ours get started?" Clara asked well-rounded and full-bearded Dr. Charles F. J. Lehlbach in the lecture room. Surely he would be a good one to ask, she thought, for had she not heard that Dr. Lehlbach's father had been with the hospital since the beginning?

Dr. Lehlbach leaned back in his chair, and surveyed the four girls, in their crisply starched blue uniforms with white aprons, sitting on straight-backed chairs before him.

"Well, it was like this," he began, lighting his pipe. His tone said, "This is a favorite subject of mine."

"Someone has said that every institution is the lengthened shadow of one great man. In the case of the German Hospital, I think we can say it is the lengthened shadow of three notable men."

He drew deeply from his pipe two or three times, then laid it on the table, made a tent with his fingers, and went on.

"All three fled from Germany during the aborted Revolution of 1848. All three had dedicated their lives to freeing the oppressed from the tyranny of the harsh German princes. All three, when they fled to America, considered themselves more exiles than immigrants. All three were educated, cultured men.

"The first was Dr. Louis Greiner, a lawyer who received his training in Munich University. He had been sentenced to death and was in prison. But somehow he escaped and fled to the U. S.

"The second was Dr. Fridalin Ill. Father told me he was only 27 when he joined the revolutionaries. He lost all his patients because of that. He too fled for safety.

"Then there was my father, Rev. Frederick August Lehlbach. When he joined the dissenters, he was arrested. I remember father telling about the day he appeared before the judge. "Fifteen years in prison!" the judge thundered and whammed down his gavel. Father said he shook all over but tried not to show it. But Father too escaped and fled to these shores. Here he became pastor of the Evangelical Protestant Church on Mulberry Street. Dr. Ill resumed his medical work here in Newark.

"Many other dissenters fled and found their way to Newark. By 1856 nearly one third of Newark's 100,00 residents were German immigrants: factory owners, factory workers, laborers, jewelry makers, brewers, and brewery workers.

"The earlier settlers of Newark, who were very puritanical in their way of life, looked sideways at the hard-living, fun-loving, beer-drinking Germans. So the Germans withdrew to the hills of Newark and jokingly dubbed their community 'Schmierkaese County' after a favorite cheese spread of their native country.

"In this community on the hill the German language filled the air, and German customs were perpetuated.

"Germantown, at that time, was an interesting city with tall, narrow buildings and industries belching smoke. Laundry flapped dry from clothes lines strung from window to window, even three or four stories up. People pulled little handcarts down the paved streets. Pigs, ducks, geese, and chickens cackled, grunted, and flapped their way around freely, while penned cattle mooed and added their own

36

pungent aroma to the surroundings."

Dr. Lehlbach paused to relight his pipe. He puffed briefly, then picked up his story.

"Time moved on. Then one day in May 1856 the editor of the Newark Daily Advertiser heard a commotion on Market Street and glanced out to see a horse and buggy come chasing down the street. The driver reined in the foaming, perspiring horse, jumped down, and ran into a doctor's office. Loud talking ensued. Then the driver dashed out the door, jumped into his wagon, and whipped his horse into action. They took off with a jerk that almost threw the driver. As they passed by, the editor saw, a man lying in the back of the wagon, his face drained of color, his eyes staring fixedly. They had ripped off his bloody coat and shirt and his right arm was lying beside him, clear out of its socket. Horrified, the editor watched the driver and wagon tear down the street a bit farther and then come to another abrupt halt. The driver jumped out, ran into a building, and was out and off again in a few minutes, with the wagon teetering as it careened around a corner. The editor, writing about the incident in his paper the next day, commented, 'We know not how long or how far the unfortunate man was obliged to travel in order to obtain the assistance which, in a dense community like this, he ought to have been able to receive with much less trouble and suffering.'"

Dr. Lehlbach stood up and leaned on the back of his chair. "At this time, you understand, most sick people were being cared for in their homes. But the poor who couldn't afford to bring medical help to their homes had to go to the City Alms House, where the insane and senile were cooped up. Conditions were so crowded that sometimes two or more had to share a bed.

"Some of the leading men in Germantown, including the three men I mentioned earlier, began to talk about building a public hospital. When the townspeople down the hill heard this, they said they wanted to build one. Things dillydallied back and forth. The townspeople talked a lot and raised some money, but that's as far as they got.

"When the Civil War broke out, the trains and ships dumped hundreds of wounded on our doorstep. An old four-story brick warehouse was requisitioned in 1862 and converted into a temporary hospital. Later, near the end of the war, a specially built hospital was constructed. When all the soldiers finally went home, that hospital was put up for sale. But do you think the townspeople bought it? Never. It went to a private company to be used for something else."

Dr. Lehlbach had been pacing, pipe cradled in his hand. He stopped now and laughed. "I can still remember the indignation of my father. He shook his snowy head so hard the little black skull cap he used to wear fell off.

"Well, the townspeople got wind that the Germans were getting restless and impatient. They wrote a letter trying to calm us down and reminding us that 'Rome was not built in a day.'

"We couldn't have cared less about Rome. What we cared about was getting a hospital built for the poor and suffering of Newark. So we went ahead, and Dec. 26, 1870, we moved into our new hospital.

"As with all private hospitals, financing always has been a problem, but, with bazaars, picnics, fairs, benefit concerts, donations, the Ladies Guild, and estates willed to us, we've pulled through."

Dr. Lehlbach stopped pacing.

"On dedication day my aged father gave the main address. I can still hear him saying, 'This German hospital will admit anybody.'" Dr. Lehlbach thumped the table with his fist for emphasis. "'This institution is organized on broad principles, admitting cheerfully the afflicted of every class,'" thump, thump, "'nationality,'" thump, thump, "'and creed,'" thump, thump. "My father and his two friends felt strongly on these issues. How could they forget how they had suffered?"

Dr. Lehlbach's voice assumed a preacher-tone.

"The founding fathers of our hospital were men committed to bringing hope and comfort to the oppressed, at any personal cost," he intoned. "They were willing to risk all in caring for others. 'The grave is secure,' one of them often quoted, 'but terribly dull. Let us live life to the full, for others—little brown brothers, or big black brothers, or grimy white brothers. All are to be cherished as God's people.'"

Dr. Lehlbach paused. He resumed his fatherly tone. "Now if you girls, our nurses, can imbibe the spirit of the founding fathers of our hospital and be willing to risk all to alleviate the suffering of others, we shall be proud of you. We shall honor you and remember you."

It had been a long, unexpected, extemporaneous lecture. The bandages Dr. Lehlbach had intended to use to demonstrate proper bandaging still lay in neat rolls on the table. He looked at his watch, then at the bandages, and smiled.

"No time for bandaging today," he said. "Never mind. Tomorrow we shall consider the bandages. That is," he added, "if caring for the patients allows us time for class. Good day, ladies."

As he started for the door, the student nurses arose and stood quietly at attention until he had walked out of the lecture room.▪

5

Clara Is Introduced
to the Yellow Bloodletter

Clara lay propped up on her elbows in bed. She had pushed her book as close to the window as possible to catch every bit of early morning light. She turned a page and sneezed unexpectedly. Her roommate stirred and opened one sleep-sodden eye.

"What test are you studying for now?" Faint annoyance.

Clara didn't move her eyes from her book. "Not a test," she said, "a report I have to give in class. About yellow fever. Found this book," she flipped back to the cover and read, "A History of the Yellow Fever: the Yellow Fever Epidemic of 1878, in Memphis, Tennessee."

"Humph! I've enough fever to take care of in the wards without thinking about it outside of class," her roommate mumbled. She rolled over and pulled the sheet up over her head.

Clara had opened her mouth to say something, but shut it and returned to her book.

The flame of the fever was licking the heart of the city, she read. The city was tipsy with jitters. It had begun when a few isolated persons began to burn with fever and shake with chills. Sunstroke, some had conjectured. But then their limbs began to ache throbbingly. Next jaundice followed. If the disease did not release its victim, the next phase was the most horrible of all. The patient would double up, then straighten out suddenly and stiffen. Then out shot a geyser of black vomit, spraying everything and everybody within its reach. The black vomit usually indicated the end of life.

The terrifying thing about the yellow fever monster was that no one knew where it came from, Clara read on. "To trap yellow fever is like trying to trap fear," one doctor declared. "We're paralyzed by our ignorance," another cried out. "I feel like a man without hands," still another, in feverish despair, ejaculated. "We doctors are not practicing medicine here, we are playing at blindman's buff. The murderous Unseen Fiend continues to prance lightly before and around us, silently smiling his death into the air, and triumphantly mocking the slow feet of our knowledge, the outstretched blind fingertips of our puny imagination."

Clara turned the page. That year of 1878, as people broiled in the August sun, cases multiplied daily. Twenty-two stricken. Two dead. A hundred more down. Fifty-six dead. New Orleans: 1,355 cases. 396 dead. Grenada: only 200 of a population of 2,200 left alive. Memphis declared: At least 3,000 now are sick. Sixty percent of the sick are dying. Yellow fever deaths to date are 2,250. Our city is a hospital. Sixteen physicians and more than 100 nurses have heroically died.

The book continued its tale.

As the deadly reports poured in, panic gripped the populace. People began to flee. Some simply walked out of their houses, carrying nothing, running for the nearby hills. Others piled onto steamboats to head north. Still others climbed into whatever vehicle they could find: carriages, wagons, buggies, furniture vans, street drays, goat-carts, handcarts, wheelbarrows—all were put into use. Roads were choked. Dust hung heavy in the air as horses and donkeys jostled for space. It was like a gigantic Roman chariot race, only there were neither rules nor referees.

Hundreds pawned silverware, watches, and jewelry and rushed to the railroad station to buy tickets. Station agents sold $30,000 worth of tickets in one week. Waiting for the trains, the people camped in the railroad stations, squatted on the platforms, and overflowed into the streets. When a train finally came whistling in, the rush was worse than any during a major department store sale. People pried open or broke the windows of the coaches and climbed in over the occupants of the seats in spite of their protestations. Around the doors the crunch was so tight no one could move. Elbows jabbed. Fists pounded heads. Shouting filled the air. Mumbling. Snarling. Clawing. Hair pulling. Oaths. Pistols were waved. Threats uttered.

The railroad workers hooked on additional cars, but they were jammed full as soon as they were on the tracks. Creaking, groaning, and protesting, the heavily laden trains finally would grunt off. A few desperate people would lunge for and grab the handrails by the steps and ride along, hanging on for their very lives.

Only one train was not bombarded. When this train pulled into the station, the people rushed for the doors—then drew back in horror. The entire train was filled with coffins!

Soon cities lay as desolate as the desert. Long rows of houses stood vacant and silent.

In most cities a goodly number of physicians stayed on. While they were in houses making calls, consternation-stricken, fleeing families would steal their horses and buggies. Soon the doctors and nurses had to tramp about on foot to do their visitation. As they walked, they often heard feeble cries for help from what had appeared to be a vacant house. On entering, they would find the dead in blood-and-vomit-soaked beds, and one or two stricken, still alive, but too weak to go for help. In some cases they discovered whole families annihilated, lying in their beds dead and decaying. "Queerly enough," a doctor wrote, "time seems extended, and sometimes I feel as though a full year is crushed into a day."

Then news began to dribble back from the fleeing trains. After they left the cities, those on the steps were pushed off or would become exhausted and fall. Doors and windows were locked tight to keep out the air from the infected areas through which they passed. On and on the trains sped, 50 miles an hour, through city after city, carrying the people farther and farther from the scenes of death.

At last, hundreds of miles away, the trains would coast to a stop at some small station, to let the people detrain, only to be greeted by frenzied townspeople, armed with pitchforks, clubs, and stones forbidding them to get off. Everybody and everything was suspect. Who knew how the disease spread?

People distrusted the night air. Street cars stopped running at sundown. Curfew was enforced after dark. Still the yellow killer lurked, sight unseen. It was eerie.

One young doctor, left in a dying city, wrote: "It is ominously quiet tonight. I looked out just now, and the sky, surprisingly, is clear, the stars shining, the air balmy, fragrant with summer. No taint of the poison, here where I am, no sound of this death."

Daily the newspapers described tragic discoveries. A man named Donahoo was taken down with fever. On the fourth day his reason left him. Invested with strength born of insanity, he jumped from his bed, drove nurses out of doors, and seized a weapon in an attempt to murder his sister.

A poor woman was found on Main Street, near the Louisville depot, in a miserable hut, sitting stiff, stark-dead in a chair, with a dead child hanging by the nipple of her left breast on which it had closed its little gums as it breathed its last.

"Fear sits on every face and dread on every heart," the editor commented. "We work in the very face of death. Hope, we have none. Our first words in the morning are, "Who lives, and who has died?'"

The need for nurses became known through the country and brought an invasion of cutthroats, thieves, and prostitutes. The large majority of those who came, came to pilfer the dead and use every other opportunity they could find to fatten their own purses by stealing or swindling. Many of them were alcoholics. Day after day the newspaper reported incidents like that of the nurse who, dead drunk, fell on top of his patient on her bed. He had been dancing around wildly, brandishing an empty wine bottle. The suffering sick lay in fear of the nurses and were at their mercy, yet they could not do without them.

Otherwise decent people became less than human. Take the case of Mr. Donovan, a man socially and politically influential and highly respected. When his pregnant wife and two children came down with the fever, he fled to another town. Telegrams pleaded with him to return. In answer he only sent instructions to hire nurses to care for his family. Another telegram came. His wife was in labor. She was calling for him. He did not respond. His wife gave birth to a stillborn child. Still he did not return. Finally she too died, and the same day one of the children. Even then he did not return for their funerals. Later when the other child died, the father was 60 miles away.

Others, however, who had seemed to be dubious characters, were born again into worthy individuals. There was Annie, the erring sister who operated a house of prostitution. She dissolved her business, converted her elegant house into a hospital, and doubled and trebled the pay of her servants to coax them to stay on to cook and clean. She hired reliable nurses and lovingly cared for all the yellow fever patients sent her, until one day the diesase seized her too and twisted life out of her. And though the city had banned all funeral processions, people disregarded it for Annie. Rich and poor, men, women, and children, all accompanied Annie's body to its grave and wept unashamedly at their irretrievable loss.

"A catastrophe like this routes out all the latent or slumbering characters of people as a flood drives out all the rabbits and gophers, the skunks and mice," one wrote. "In a day or an hour the traits buried or lurking unsuspected in men, both the good and the bad, the heroic and the craven, come to light. The mild clerk leaps into the breach where his comrade falls, and faces the enemy seemingly without fear. The frail widow tearlessly buries her dead and then shoulders the labors of an Amazon. The notorious scoundrel suddenly steps out of his villainy and unselfishly shows virtuous courage."

Another bright spot was the foundation of a nucleus of caring people who chose to stay on to care for the stricken and bury the dead. They chose "The Howards" as their name, after John Howard, 18th-century English philanthropist, who initiated notable prison reforms. "God knows it's repulsive to see human beings rotting with yellow jack," one Howard said, "but this craven scurrying of mice masquerading as men shrinks the dignity of all of us."

With the exodus of hundreds, businesses folded. Unemployment followed. Hunger began to pinch people's stomachs. Greedy men looted abandoned homes. Jailers died, and there was no choice but to open the prison doors and turn the prisoners loose. People from other areas sent down food for relief, but were not enough well people to distribute it.

Funeral services were abandoned. The living were caring for the sick. "All of Sunday and yesterday, hearses followed each other at a trot to the cemetery," one newspaper article declared, "unattended by any but the drivers. Even this was not fast enough, and corpses accumulated in various parts of the city, until the fearful stench became alarmingly offensive."

Trenches were dug, and the dead were buried five deep. "Where sorrow is so general," one wrote, "there can be no individual solemnities; the city itself is a funeral party."

"The sense of feeling has gone," another wrote. "The eyes have wept until the fountain has gone dry."

"Our people have lost all appearance of panic," yet another newspaper announced. "They are now coolly awaiting 'their turn,' as it were, like the soldier who goes out on picket, knowing not whether he will ever meet his comrades again."

As late summer 1878 wore on, the scourge, which had been scorching the South, moved northward to Cairo, Ill.; St. Louis, Mo.; New Albany, N. Y.; Cincinnati, Ohio; Pittsburgh, Pa.; and Norfolk, Va. Even certain cities of Indiana were invaded. By sea the killer moved up the Delaware to Philadelphia, Pa., up the Chesapeake to Baltimore, Md., and up the Potomac to Washington, D. C. By late summer the fever had invaded 132 towns, producing a loss of 15,932 lives out of a total number of cases that reached more than 74,000. New Orleans alone totaled more than 4,600 deaths.

Loss of life was but part of the distress. Reliable sources announced that $4,500,000 had been sent from unaffected areas for relief. Financial losses in the afflicted cities rose steadily, reaching $100,000,000. New Orleans alone wailed she had lost $10,000,000. The Southern Pacific Railroad in Texas and Louisiana declared a loss of over $1,000,000.

Everybody everywhere was praying for frost, the only thing they knew that would stop the bloodletter. Frost in August! Only a miracle could bring this.—

Clara's roommate was stirring. With a start Clara realized that the sun was streaming through the windows in full strength. A brisk breeze wafted the aroma of coffee and bacon in from the hospital kitchen. Clara shut her book, got up, washed, and dressed absentmindedly. Habit, not hunger, sent her to the dining hall. She silently picked her way through breakfast.

In the hospital, as she made rounds, she automatically made beds, gave baths, emptied bedpans, and checked temperatures. So preoccupied was she, that she did not even notice that the bed of the typhoid patient was empty. Only at lunch did she realize what had happened when she heard one of the girls say, "So sad! Forty-four days burning up with fever, and then, when it drops to 100 degrees, he dies."

Suddenly Clara felt a slow anger building up in her—anger against all the diseases that attack humans and destroy them—anger at typhoid fever, which had consumed another brave man who had fought so hard and so long against it—anger at the yellow fever she had read about, that sneak, silently attacking and often shedding blood.

"Is there no way?" she puzzled. "No way to conquer these murderers?" She dug her clenched fingers deep into the palms of her hands. And then, even as her anger burned hot and fierce, a shiver rippled through her slight frame. A chilling premonition swept over her, a premonition that the battle to conquer these

46

fevers would be only at a fearful cost, not only to one, but to many, and the cost may well be lives. But little did Clara guess that one day it would involve her too.■

6

Cap and Pin and Ready to Go

One of the student nurses was in tears. Fever was raging in a patient who had submitted to an appendectomy, and she was being blamed for it. The doctor, making his rounds, had cussed and sworn when he removed the bandages from the man's incision and had seen the long cut red and inflamed, oozing greenish-yellow pus. As the doctor cleaned and redressed the wound he scolded the nurse with bitter, caustic words. His deep voice thundered out the door and down the hall. Clara and another nurse, on their way to answer lights, stopped momentarily, looked at each other, and shook their heads.

"It wasn't my fault," the nurse wailed to Clara later when they met in the parlor at Trefz Hall. "I know everybody around here says our doctors have been some of the first to adopt and follow Lister's theory in regard to antiseptics. But this doctor seldom washes his hands before he makes rounds and checks wounds. And then who gets the blame if the patient gets an infection? Not the doctor—oh, no—but the poor nurse."

"Have you seen yesterday's paper?" Clara asked. "Our Dr. Ill addressed the annual meeting of the New Jersey Medical Society. You'll be interested in reading what he said. Here—wait a minute—I'll run and get the paper for you."

A couple of minutes later Clara reappeared with the newspaper under her arm and a cup of coffee in her hand.

"Here, now," she said, "just sit down and drink this coffee while I read to you."

She opened the paper. Her eyes scanned the columns. "Here it is," she said, holding the paper closer. "Listen to what Dr. Ill said to all these people.

> There is probably no innovation in the practice of medicine during the past thirty years save the adoption of aseptic surgery, which has so altered conditions and has been of such great value as the creation of the trained nurse. We owe her much, and many a practitioner would not care to practice medicine without her help. . . . But just as we educate her and just as we set an example so will she do her work. It will be wise to look for any fault in the nurse to ourselves first. In her education in the hospital she must find only models of neat, clean, and conscientious doctors. She should learn, and I assure you quickly learn, to single out the black sheep among us. The proper start for her work depends on us. We cannot expect more of the nurse than of the doctor. A puerperal infection, placed at the door of the nurse when the doctor made his examination with unwashed hands, is a deplorable and frequent occurrence and does not tend to elevate the respect, which the nurse should hold us in. . . . To whom shall the nurse look for example and truth if it be not to him who teaches the coming generation of medical men?

"There, doesn't that make you feel better?" Clara asked. "You see, all our doctors aren't like the one who exploded today."

"But I just know I'll never be able to pass all those exams," the student said, bursting into tears again.

"There, there," soothed Clara, slipping an arm around the girl's shaking shoulders. "I was feeling down one day. Dr. Ill noticed and stopped to talk. 'I understand how you feel,' he said. 'When I was a young medical student, I had the same worries. I didn't know how I'd ever make it through all the years of study. Then one day a doctor said I should set my goal, then forget it, and take each day as it came. I did. I filled each day as full as I could and did the best I could, and what happened? I stopped worrying and achieved my goal.'"

Clara rubbed the young girl's back. "That's what I'm trying to do," she said. "My goal is to become the best nurse I can and live a worthwhile, significant life. But I give my energy to the work of the day, whatever it is: cooking, cleaning, nursing, or studying."

The girl blew her nose, dabbed at her eyes, and smiled crookedly at Clara.

"Why don't you dash some cold water on your eyes?" Clara suggested. "And then we better get back to the wards."

There were heartaches and anxieties for the student nurses, but also much for which to thank God. Clara realized this more and more as the days went on. Of the 49 appendectomy patients between 1892 and 1900 only 9 died. That percentage today would be considered an extremely high mortality rate. But in a day when a ruptured appendix killed, the emphasis was on the number of lives saved, not lost.

Eagerly Clara waited for the time when she would be allowed to observe surgeries. Finally the day came.

Clara was conscious of her heart thumping as she walked into the operating room. Black and white block tiles covered the floor. Everything else was white. White enameled cupboards and carts. White walls. White enameled pails on the floor. White sinks. High white stools. White enameled steel operating table.

Clara watched with fascination as the gowned doctors took up their positions around the patient on the operating table. She saw the instruments soaking in carbolic acid. The anesthetist, seated at the head of the table, guided and controlled the intake of ether. To her surprise, the doctors talked freely and even jested as they went about their work.

Looking at the draped patient lying immobile and unfeeling, Clara tried to imagine what it had been like before the days of ether. She remembered the story of brave Mrs. Jane Todd Crawford, who had consented to have Dr. Ephraim McDowell cut her open and pry loose and lift from her a 22-pound tumor—all with the aid of only a little morphine to help deaden some of the pain. Clara shuddered as she thought of it. What a breakthrough anesthetics had been!

Clara's thoughts wandered back to the lecture on Morton's discovery of ether. She had thought it strange that the discovery had come about the way it had. Morton, a student in dentistry, was with some partying friends who were sniffing sulfuric ether for kicks. He noticed that those high on the drug, in lighting their cigarettes or pipes would let the matches burn down to their fingers and seemingly not feel the pain. One of them, slicing bread, cut himself rather badly. He too did not wince from pain. Questions began to pop into Morton's mind. Did ether deaden pain? If it did, couldn't it be used for surgeries?

He began to experiment with mice. Excited about the results, he asked the surgeon general at the Massachusetts General Hospital if he could try the drug on the next surgical patient. The surgeon consented.

As Morton administered the ether, the team stood tense, watching attentively, their eyes beadlike on the patient. The patient's eyes fluttered shut. His chest rose and fell gently. His deep, even breathing filled the room. The surgeon put the knife to his flesh. All craned their necks forward. A thin trickle of blood followed the line of the knife. The patient did not stir but slept on. Afterwards his recovery was much faster than usual and more pain-free.

An angry outburst from one of the doctors startled Clara out of her reverie. "Can't you ever learn to hand me the right instruments?" the doctor yelled. Clara shivered. It wouldn't do to daydream when her turn came to assist the doctors, she thought. She shifted. Her feet hurt from standing still so long on the tile floor. "If we can discover ether to deaden the pain of the knife, why can't we make shoes comfortable?" she wondered.

Later that day she bumped into one of the doctors in the hall. Face reddening, she stammered an apology. The doctor smiled with amusement and then asked, "Well, how did you enjoy your first day in surgery?"

"It was fascinating!" Clara's dancing blue eyes behind her rimless glasses were shining. "I was thinking how wonderful it is we have anesthetics."

"Ah, yes!" the doctor agreed. "Because of ether we have been able to do so many more really difficult surgeries. Did you know that we doctors here from our hospital have been the first in the U. S. to perform stomach resection and do cesarean section? We also did the first successful operation for resection of the bowel." The pride in his tone was evident.

The pride the doctor had felt in their accomplishments in the hospital was as contagious as a yawn, for as Clara continued down the wall on her way to the wards, she found herself walking taller and humming softly. And as she nursed her patients, she alternately comforted or teased gently, her voice vibrating with joy and confidence.

Transfer to the obstetrical ward brought added delight and satisfaction, and, with it, a brief period of lightened duties gave opportunity for a little extra and much-needed rest. While mothers still preferred to have their babies at home, little by little more and more were choosing to come to the hospital. On the average, a baby every two weeks squalled his or her arrival. The atmosphere, on the whole, in the mother-and-baby ward, was sunny. The success of cesarean sections extended hope to parents who before had grieved over babies born dead. In some cases, previously, the mother too had died; now the mother's life also was spared.

Little by little, as the weeks passed, Clara learned to let her thoughts rest on all the alleviation of pain and the remarkable recoveries that hospital care made possible. Even when patients died, Clara knew comfort and loving care made their last days easier. As she concentrated on these aspects, she no longer felt overwhelmed by all the uncurable diseases. Her helplessness in the face of them was buoyed by the assurance that some day someone would find something that would help. In the meantime, she would do all she could to create the conditions and atmosphere her patients needed for recovery. She threw herself into her work, and as she did, she found her joy multiplying.

The German hospital matched her buoyant spirit on Sept. 1 and 2, 1895. At that time the directors and supporters of the hospital, together with the townspeople, who now grudgingly acknowledged the worth of the hospital, joyously celebrated the 25th birthday of the hospital. Hundreds gathered in Caledonia Park and opened the Sunday morning festivities with a sparkling musical program. Seven hundred blended their voices in a mass choir. The Newark Zither Club played several numbers, and five Turnvereins tumbled as they entertained with gymnastics.

On Monday the people lined the streets to watch a "Grand Festival Parade" from downtown to Caledonia Park. At the park they patiently listened to two addresses, one in German and one in English, knowing afterwards they would be free to bowl, to participate in shooting matches, and to celebrate merrily until late at night.

The English and German languages were mixed up happily, not only in the conversation that floated in the air but in the printed anniversary programs. The cover and the advertisements were in English, the program in German. This combination of languages foretold a coming change when peoples other than Germans would join the hospital staff and later when even the name of the German hospital would be changed.

For all the gaiety of that celebration and for all the joyous satisfaction Clara was discovering in her work, still it was with solemn face on Oct. 12, 1895, that she repeated the Florence Nightingale pledge:

> I solemnly pledge myself before God and in the presence of this assembly to pass my life in purity and to practice my profession faithfully.
>
> I will abstain from whatever is deleterious and mischievous, and will not take or knowingly administer any harmful drug. I will do all in my power to maintain and elevate the standard of my profession, and will hold in confidence all personal matters committed to my keeping and all family affairs coming to my knowledge in the practice of my calling.

> With loyalty will I endeavor to aid the physician in his work and
> devote myself to the welfare of those committed to my care.

Then 19-year-old Clara stood very still while the director of nursing placed the white muslin cap with the tiny pleats and the narrow black ribbon over Clara's soft hair, curled for the occasion. Under Clara's chin, at the base of the stiff round collar of her crisp uniform, the director of nursing fastened the nursing pin of the German Hospital.

The seemingly endless, tedious years of working, first as a mother's helper in many homes and later in the children's orphanage, suddenly were worthwhile. Those years had prepared her for the hard work and long hours her nurse's training had demanded. Now she stood, equipped and trained, on the threshold of a new adventure.

Clara chose, however, to begin her career in familiar surroundings. She stayed on at the German Hospital, augmenting her skimpy salary with wages earned as she worked additional hours as private duty nurse in homes. So faithful and conscientious was she and so skilled in her nursing, that in less than three years the hospital directors elevated her to the position of head nurse.

As head nurse, with student nurses working under her, Clara now found herself in the teaching position Florence Nightingale had filled much of her life. Now, like Florence had done before her, Clara had to remind the student nurses, for example, that if they didn't empty bedpans and chamber pots frequently they "might as well have a sewer under the room."

"Cleanliness in every respect is of utmost importance," she would stress.

"Prevention is better than cure," was another phrase she would repeat over and over.

Many were the lessons, learned in the classroom, that she passed on.

"We must retain our ideals. At the same time we must be willing and able to change methods.

"We need to learn to work as teammembers. The doctor, the

nurse, the patient, and the drugs—all work together.

"All times, as nurses, we consider the welfare of our patients. We nurse people, not diseases. A good nurse not only cares for people but cares about them.

"We need to obey those above us," she would remind the girls. "But we must obey intelligently, using discretion, not obeying blindly. Even the wisest can make mistakes.

"Nursing is an art. The health of the soul and the health of the body are equally important, both for you and for your patient."

One day as Clara sat in the kitchen enjoying a cup of tea with a student nurse, she kindly cautioned the student against making excessive noise.

"Nurses have to learn to keep their voices pitched low and to open and shut doors quietly," she said. "They should learn to walk with a firm, light, quick step. At the same time we have to learn not to tiptoe into the room so quietly that we startle the patient."

The student laughed. "With our rustling crinoline skirts I don't see how anyone could not hear us coming."

Clara laughed too. "I know. I'm afraid I feel the same way Florence Nightingale does about these skirts. Florence, I am told, used to fume and protest that it would be much more sensible if women nurses could wear the pants the male nurses did. She feels women's long dresses are totally unfitted for ease in doing any kind of housework or nursing. 'What is become of woman's light step?' she has asked. 'A woman now either shuffles or waddles.'" And jumping up, Clara simulated, first a slow shuffle and then a side-to-side sweeping waddle, to the amusement of the student nurse.

Sitting down again Clara said, "It isn't easy for women to do some of the things they really would like to do." She refilled her cup.

"As women, we're tied in to certain stereotype pictures people have of us. Did you ever hear or read about Dr. James Barry, who died just 11 years before I was born? Dr. Barry was known as an outstanding surgeon in the British army. Small in stature, of slight build, and with a rather squeaky voice, he was pugnacious, quick-tempered, and sensitive to any kidding or teasing. If anyone twitted him about the fact that he couldn't grow a beard, he'd fly into a rage and challenge them to a duel. After he had served with the army for over 50 years and only after he died and they were preparing his body for burial, did they discover that Dr. Barry was, in reality, a woman and one who had given birth to at least one child. But the leadership at the British Medical Association and the officials at the War Office were so embarrassed that on Dr. Barry's death certificate and gravestone she was still decreed to be a he."

The student chuckled. "It hasn't been easy for women to enter the medical field, has it?"

"No," Clara sighed, "especially not if women wanted to train to be doctors. The Quakers and certain doctors have tried to gain admission for women into medical schools, but it hasn't been easy. In 1850 Harriot Hunt tried to enter Harvard Medical School. Oliver Wendell Holmes, dean of the school, agreed to let her attend lectures, but he warned her that no degree could be conferred. And when she actually showed up in the classroom, the male students rioted, and Harriot had to abandon her dreams.

"With nursing it has been different. Down through the centuries nursing has been one profession which, more or less, has been open to both men and women. In ancient Ceylon and Persia, men as well as women served as nurses, and slaves often were trained as nurses. But then, interestingly enough, in Greece, when a male slave nurse became ill, it was the wealthy mistress of that house that nursed the sick slave. Quite a turnaround. Slaves, you see, were considered the most valuable property a person owned."

"We must not forget either," Clara added, "the mighty impetus the Christian church gave to nursing, following the example of Christ, who healed."

"Nursing is really a wide-open field for girls now, isn't it?" the student asked.

"In most cases, yes. We can thank Florence Nightingale for that. She, more than any other single person, has made nursing a highly respected profession.

56

"But I suspect it's still rough going in certain situations. I wonder, for example, just how well female nurses are received in the armed forces. But we must be patient. Give us a few more years, and we'll make a name for ourselves.

Little did Clara realize, as she spoke those words, how she herself would one day make a name for herself. Nor did she understand that the national events pyramiding daily were setting the stage for her sacrifice.■

7

Clara Voices a Daring Decision

It was February 1898. "Look at this!" One of the nurses had the newspaper spread open on the parlor table in Trefz Hall. "My father fought in the Civil War. Now it looks as though he'll be going to war again."

Splashed across the front page of the Journal was the news of the U. S. battleship Maine having been blow up Feb. 15 in Havana harbor. Two hundred sixty-six men had been blown to bits with the ship.

"Do you think Spain was responsible?" Clara asked. "Or was it an accident?"

"No doubt that Spain did it," one of the girls declared authoritatively. "Haven't you been reading the papers? All the stories of tyranny and harsh feudalistic treatment the Spaniards have been afflicting on the Cubans? Now they're starting to give us the same treatment. We should have been in there long ago, setting the Cubans free."

"Trouble's been brewing a long time in Cuba," Clara admitted. "Some say the Spaniards haven't developed the country. Sugar is their main product, and when the market for sugar slumps, the entire economy of the country nose-dives."

One of the younger students spoke up. "I remember from history class reading about the revolt in 1869 when the insurrectionists declared independence. Civil War raged for 10 years. A treaty finally ended it. But Spain never introduced the reforms the treaty called for except for setting the slaves free."

"When a treaty's not met," the first student said, folding up the paper, "there's bound to be trouble."

"There was. Civil war erupted again in 1885, and again just three years ago."

"Do you really believe all the stories in the paper are true?" Clara was speaking.

The girls look startled.

"Why do you ask?"

"Well, take that story about the American girl who was searched on the ship Olivette. Remember the sketch?"

The girls nodded. "You mean the one whom the Spaniards thought was concealing rebel literature on her body?"

"I remember the sketch! It showed this pretty young girl standing naked in her cabin while three Spanish officers searched her clothing, only remember—where were those guys looking? Not at her clothes—no sirree! Wasn't it awful?"

"Well, now," Clara said heatedly, "the truth was something else. Some days later, after the Olivette had docked in New York, I read an article in the World that refuted the story the Journal had carried. The World sent a reporter right to the ship. What did he discover? Not one young lady, but three middle-aged ladies. Yes, they had been searched, but by a policewoman, not by three men. The cabin was locked, not standing with open door. The portholes were covered, not open, and a guard stood outside the locked door to prevent anyone from entering. But did the editors of the Journal correct their story? Not on your life! Why? I think because they want to stir up hatred towards the Spaniards and fling us into war."

The girls had been listening, mouths hanging open.

"Why was the Maine lying off Havana harbor in the first place?" one of the girls asked.

"Oh, I can explain that," Clara said. "There are U. S. citizens in Cuba. The U. S. sent the Maine to lie ready to evacuate them if things really got serious. But how can they be sure a Spanish-placed mine caused the explosion? That's what I would like to know?"

"I expect there'll be an investigation committee appointed," one of the girls said.

There was. President McKinley pleaded for calmness and sanity. He appointed a U. S. naval court to make thorough investigations. Spain protested her innocence in the affair and asked that she be allowed to participate in the investigations.

Clara and the other nurses were discussing it at supper one night.

"Why should they be allowed to sit in on the investigations?" one of the girls said excitedly, knocking over a glass of water as she waved her hands about. She ran for a cloth. "It's very clear they're guilty. I think we should get down to Cuba and fight!"

One of the girls giggled. "Did you read Teddy Roosevelt's remarks about President McKinley? He said President McKinley has no more backbone than a chocolate éclair." She giggled again.

"President McKinley wants to negotiate," Clara said. "He wants to know why Spain can't give Cuba the same position Great Britain gave Canada."

"It'll never work. The only language Spain will understand is rat-a-tat-tat language from guns. Our guns. I think we should get down there right away."

The student nurse was not alone in her feverish cry. All over the United States people picked up the chant, "Remember the Maine," and "Independence for Cuba." The chorus swelled louder and louder and grew into a thunderous roar. Petitions for war poured into Washington. Under pressure, on May 9, the Congress appropriated $50,000,000 for "national defense." The navy was assembled at Key West. Orders went out to the warship, <u>Oregon,</u> one of the newest of the fleet, to steam out of San Francisco Bay and proceed to the West Indies via the Strait of Magellan.

With consternation Spain learned of these advances and remonstrated. But on March 25 the Court of Inquiry heard 12,000 typed pages of testimony and gave this decision to the public:

> . . . the loss of the <u>Maine</u> was not in any respect due to fault or negligence on the part of the officers or members of the crew, . . . the ship was destroyed by the explosion of a submarine mine.

Spain had conducted its own investigation and protested that the explosion was internal and presumably accidental or spontaneous.

But the people of the U. S. had neither ears to hear nor a heart for peaceful settlement. War! War! War! went up the cry.

The evening of April 20 a small group of nurses huddled together in the parlor at Trefz Hall, devouring the copy of the <u>Journal</u> that lay spread before them. The resolutions Congress had passed the day before were spelled out. They read in part:

> Resolved . . . that the people of the Island of Cuba are, and of a right out to be, free and independent.
> Second, That it is the duty of the U. S. to demand and the Government of Spain at once to relinquish its authority and government in the Island of Cuba . . .
> Third, That the President of the U. S. be, and he hereby is, directed and empowered to use the entire land and naval forces of the U. S. . . . to such an extent as may be necessary to carry these resolutions into effect.

"There it is! We're in war!" one of the girls gasped, as they came to that part.

The girls sat silent for a while, trying to absorb what this really meant.

The silence was broken when Clara quietly announced, "If they'll accept nurses, I'm going. Not because I believe in war, but because I believe in saving lives, not in blowing them to bits. The wounded and the ill will need me, and I'm going." ■

TOP: Clara Maass' contract from the War Department; CENTER LEFT: Clara Maass (right) with Sophie File in front of Maass home in East Orange, 1899; CENTER RIGHT: Ambulance bringing sick men to field hospital; BOTTOM: Clara Maass (right standing) during her tour of duty as an Army Nurse.

8

Into the Thick of It

I've applied!" Clara announced at breakfast in Trefz Hall one morning several weeks later. "Nurses can't enlist, but Dr. Anita Newcomb McGee has sent out a call for contract nurses. Goodness knows, though, if I'll qualify."

The girls stared at Clara, then broke into excited questioning.

"You did?!"

"You actually applied?"

"Who can go? What qualifications are necessary? Maybe I should apply."

Clara produced a sheet of paper from the pocket of her apron.

"They want a statement from the school from which the applicant has graduated," she began.

"That rules me out. I've still another year left."

"They want a transcript of grades," Clara continued, "and a certificate of good reputation."

"That rules me out," another joked. Clara ignored the remark and went on.

"I've sent it all off. Now I've only to wait until I hear."

"They'll accept you, Clara," the girls encouraged. "If you don't get in, who will?" Then, "Will you stay on here until you receive word?"

"I've talked to the matron about that and offered to stay on without salary."

"Without salary?"

"I wouldn't dream of expecting the hospital to pay me when I might walk out on them any day."

"When do you think you'll be going?"

"I don't know—I wish I did." Clara laughed a little excitedly. "I hope it won't be too long. Things are moving so fast."

"I know. Who ever would have dreamed that when the war was only 10 days old Commodore Dewey would sink the entire Spanish Asiatic fleet off Manila?"

"I know. Twelve ships, gurgle, gurgle, gurgle, consigned to the mud of Manila's harbor."

"Word's out," Clara said, "that by July there will be 10,000 troops in Manila."

"And there's Cuba too. And Puerto Rico."

"I hope too many won't get killed or wounded." This from one of the youngest student nurses.

"If this war is like other wars," Clara said, "not nearly as many will die from wounds as from diseases. That worries me."

One of the girls glanced at the big clock on the wall and jumped up so fast she tipped over her chair.

"I'm going to be late on duty," she called, dashing off. And two minutes later the kitchen of Trefz Hall was empty.

Day after day and week after week, as Clara waited for word, the Journal and the World exploded with news of the war.

From all over the country eager volunteers had formed regiments, the papers announced. The volunteer regiments had commandeered trains and headed south. Theodore Roosevelt had issued a call for "young, good shots, and good riders." In response,

64

ranchers, hunters, mining prospectors, cowboys, and Indians—
Cherokees, Chickasaws, Choctaws, and Creeks—had come riding
out of the far West. "They are a splendid set of men," Roosevelt
commented. "Tall and sinewy, with resolute, weather-beaten faces,
and eyes that look a man straight in the face without flinching."

"Have you ever thought what a mixed group you'll be
nursing?" one of the girls asked Clara one night as they were
walking home from church. "The first call was for those immune to
yellow fever. Blacks generally are considered immune, although
whether or not they actually are I wonder if anybody really knows.
But you'll have blacks. And then Teddy Roosevelt's wild men from
the West." She giggled. "Did you read some of their nicknames:
'Tough Ike,' 'The Dude,' 'Metropolitan Bill,' 'Pork Chop,' 'Hell
Roarer,' and 'Prayerful James.' "

Clara was serious. "I'll only try to be true to the tradition of our
hospital," she said. "Remember our hospital was dedicated to the
philosophy that all of every class, nationality, and creed shall be
admitted and cared for cheerfully."

The young student looked at her. "You sound so holy when
you say that," she objected. "I'll bet it won't be as easy as you
think."

Clara drew her eyebrows together in a frown, then relaxed and
laughed. "Maybe," she agreed.

In June, Clara learned that 18,000 soldiers had attacked
Santiago from the land side. In Trefz Hall the girls huddled again
around the newspaper, reading accounts of shooting and bayonet
charges. A sketch pictured the aftermath of an attack: a deserted
field on the edge of the woods, scattered liberally with corpses of
man and bloated horses, while vultures flapped down to pick their
way through the carcasses.

"It's horrible!" one of the girls exclaimed, putting both her
hands down to cover the picture. "You're sure you still want to go,
Clara?"

"Of course! If only I'd hear."

June dragged on into July. On July 3 the Spanish fleet, trying to flee from Cuba, was intercepted and destroyed by American ships.

And then July 16, four months after war had been declared, it appeared to be all over. Santiago surrendered.

"Won't you be going after all?" the girls asked Clara.

"I don't know." A faint trace of worry and disappointment tinged her voice.

But early fall the call came. With trembling hands Clara ripped open the envelope that bore the return address of the War Department.

"To Florida," she read, "to the field hospital of the Seventh U. S. Army Corps at Jacksonville, Florida."

"Then you won't be going to Cuba after all?"

"I guess not." Faint disappointment. "But Florida will be an adventure too."

Clara packed in a flurry, said good-bye to hospital friends and family, and boarded a train for the South.

The weather was unseasonably hot. The red plush seats made her feel hotter. Clara dropped down the windows into the slots on the side of the train. Cinders and soot sifted in. Clara was amused to see the faces of her fellow passengers turn grimy and black, cut through with little white rivers where the perspiration trickled down. Then it occurred to her that maybe she looked the same. A peek in the mirror from her handbag confirmed it. In fact, the white spots around her eyes, where her glasses shielded her face from the dirt, made her look like a clown. She got out her handkerchief, spit on it, and tried to rub her face clean, but all she got out of it was a dirty handkerchief.

Toward evening, when they pulled into a station, she took her little tin kettle and ran up to the engine for boiling water to pour over her tea leaves. Then she settled down with her bread and cheese and tea and ate her supper.

At night there were few enough passengers so she could swing around the seat in front of her, so it faced her. Then she put her suitcase in between the two seats, put her bedroll on top of the suitcase, and curled up on the two seats.

Sleep was a long time coming. The wheels of the train beat a rhythmical clack, clack, clack, bearing her farther and farther south.

The evening of the fourth day the conductor called out, "Jacksonville! Everybody getting off at Jacksonville be ready!"

A military man with a horse and buggy met her at the station. They didn't have far to go because Camp Cuba Libre, Clara was surprised to discover, was situated close to the rail terminals and lumber yards. The fresh smell of new lumber and sawdust greeted them as they drove into camp. Clara gazed with awe at the huge field filled with row after row of white tents. Here and there she saw groups of men in blue, heavy woolen uniforms standing in clumps around open campfires. The church steeples and smokestacks of the industries of the city lay off in the distance.

"Major General Fitzhugh Lee chose this place mighty carefully," her guide explained to her. "He had garnered experience from the Civil War. He wanted to be near a lumber yard so he could put floors in the tents right away and get the men off the damp ground. And see those pipes? He tied in with the city's water system too and brought water in right away. Yessir, Miss, this camp is the best of the lot, I'll bet. Notice the soil? Nice and sandy and absorbent, isn't it? When it rains, like it does every day almost, the rain just gets lost in that sand, and we don't have no mud. Originally we was supposed to be at Tampa, but Tampa got too crowded, so we was sent here. Thirty thousand of us."

He yanked back on his reins. His horse whinnied and stopped in front of a long tent. He jumped down, whirled his reins around a post, and then helped Clara dismount.

"You're real lucky, Miss," he said, squirting tobacco juice at the hitching post. "There are three other females in this camp—and here they come," he said, looking down the trail that ran between the tents. "I reckon they've been waitin' for you to arrive."

Clara greeted the three nurses from Pennsylvania with whom she would share a tent. Lucy Vandling came from Williamsport. Utilie Scheerer and Minnie Lennox were both from Philadelphia. Lucy and Minnie were about her age, Clara guessed. Utilie was older.

Laughingly Clara walked with the girls to the tent that was to become their home. A brisk wind had sprung up, and the flag flying over their tent crackled and snapped in the wind. Two soldiers stood stiffly at attention at either side of the tent, unsmiling and immobile.

"They're here to protect us," Minnie whispered, once they were inside the tent. "Some of the officers are right skitterish about having women in camp."

"Imagine," Lucy kept her voice down, "the officer who took down all my information the day I came, told me to be sure my ankles didn't show—ever."

Clara lifted her skirt and stuck her foot out. "What on earth is so dangerous about any ankle, I'd like to know," she said. "I wish we could chop our skirts off short. It'd be so much easier to get around. Especially in this—potato patch."

"Potato Patch! That's it! That's what we'll call our new home," Minnie declared.

So the girls lettered out a big sign and pinned it on one side of their tent. Across from it they pinned the name of their camp: Camp Cuba Libre.

"How are conditions?" Clara asked the next day as she walked with Minnie to the hospital tent.

Minnie shrugged. "Could be better. Could be worse. Lots of dysentery, malaria, and typhoid fever."

"I've cared for all those in the German Hospital. Food?"

"So, so. Plenty of it, but monotonous. For breakfast, bacon and beef, and bread and coffee. The soldiers have nicknamed the bacon 'sowbelly' because it's mostly lard. For dinner, beef stew. When we can get the meat fresh, it's pretty good. The stuff in the cans is rotten. We get tomatoes too, and beans and then some more bread, usually hardtack at noon. Trying to get us used to it, I guess. For supper, more bacon, bread and coffee. Trouble with the bacon is it's so hot here it gets rancid and tastes old. And the men who cook don't know how to cook. Sometimes the food is all right, but sometimes it's terrible."

"Otherwise everything seems to be orderly," Clara observed.

"It is now," Minnie agreed. "To begin with we had trouble getting supplies, and the men were eating with their fingers and using shingles and pieces of board from the lumber yard for plates. But that didn't last too long. We have plenty of tin cups and plates now. Major General Fitzhugh Lee knows how to manage things right, no question about that. You'll be right comfortable, I think. That is, if you can stand the food day after day and the long hours."

Long hours there were, for illnesses had laid flat many of the boys. Day after day and night after night Clara moved up and down the rows of cots, nursing, listening, cheering, and encouraging. Little time was spent in the Potato Patch tent aside from a few hours snatched each night to sleep on her narrow army cot.

But if they thought they had sickness to contend with, it was nothing like Santiago, Clara decided. The newspapers that the soldiers brought back with them from town ran five to six columns describing in detail the misery, illness, and disease among the troops at Santiago. Earnest pleas were going out daily for doctors and nurses. "Why don't they send us?" Clara asked. "Wouldn't we be needed there more than here?"

"I expect," Utilie said, "that one of these days we'll be getting moving orders. One of the officers here was telling me our unit was slated to have been sent to Havana this autumn for combat, but that never came off. Santiago brought the whole war to an end. But he thinks we'll be sent there for occupation. And if the unit goes, we'll go with them."

A few weeks later moving orders did come, but to Savannah, Ga. The girls were to work in the 1,000-bed base hospital that Surgeon General Sternberg had ordered constructed to serve the occupation forces of the Caribbean.

Savannah, Clara discovered, could get bitterly cold. Their wood allowance ran short. The men shivered, and the nurses hunted in vain for enough blankets to keep them warm. Day after day it rained.

One Saturday night a 60-mile-an-hour windstorm howled through camp. To begin with, the girls lay huddled under their blankets, listening to the canvas of their tent flap. When they heard the rain begin to patter on the canvas, they got up and pulled their cots away from the edges of the tent to keep their bedding dry. But as the rain pelted down more heavily, the driving wind forced the rain in under the tent walls. The girls grabbed their satchels and shoes and piled everything on top of their cots and then sat, wrapped in blankets, waiting for morning. When morning wanly dawned, they pulled aside their tent flap and looked out on a wet world and a campground in confusion. Twisted tent poles stood naked. Tents that had been ripped from their poles lay scattered across the field in careless disregard. Cots were exposed, bedding soaked, and men huddled together in disconsolate groups.

"Why can't we go home?" one young private asked. "The war's over."

"They still need occupation troops in Cuba," Clara said. "Besides, if they sent you home now, they're afraid you'd carry the fevers north with you."

"You mean," the boy exploded, "we're going to have to stay here until we are a disease-free camp—or dead?"

Georgia also introduced Clara to the poverty of the blacks and to racial prejudice. As a nurse back in Newark, she had earned $40 a month. She was aghast when she learned that blacks working in the fields earned only 35¢ a day, and cooks for private familes received only $5 a month.

The discrimination she witnessed distressed her. One day a black soldier and a white one tangled in a fist fight. The black soldier, Clara learned later, was fined $75 and thrown in the stockade, while the white soldier went free.

She was astonished also when two of their hospital tents were requisitioned to be converted into mess halls, one for black officers and one for white officers. She watched with disbelief as separate sinks were constructed for the blacks.

She listened to black soldiers complain that when they took their clothes to a steam laundry they were told, "this laundry is for the exclusive purpose of white people's work and we do nothing whatever for colored people."

At first she couldn't believe it when black soldiers told her that

70

when they got passes to town they had to stand on corners and wait and wait for special streetcars for colored people to come, even though white people's cars with only half a dozen passengers regularly passed them.

Even more horrifying were the reports of punishment meted out to black girls and women who had committed slight offenses. With ball and chain clanking around their ankles, bruising the flesh and causing huge sores, they were forced to work in chain gangs, as street cleaners, and as garbage collectors.

Observing and listening to all this, disillusionment depressed the sensitive, conscientious girl nurse from the German Hospital of Newark. She began to suspect that many in her beloved country did not subscribe to the philosophy on which her hospital had been built, that care be given cheerfully and without discrimination to all, regardless of race, creed, or color. It troubled her. She found herself responding in sympathy to those who were being put down continually.

Meanwhile, news from Santiago continued to be distressing. In August all the men of the Fifth Corps were sent back to the U. S. to 5,000 acres at Montauk Point, the eastern tip of Long Island. There they would be kept until they had recovered from their fevers.

The transfer was being badly handled, the papers protested. The troops had arrived at Montauk before the tents were up. Confusion reigned. Sick men tottered off ships only to collapse under trees and lie there exposed to wind and storm.

"The troops were dying in Cuba. We had to bring them north fast," some of the officers protested.

"But we didn't have enough time to prepare," the War Department complained. "We'll do all we can now."

And they sent out calls for more contract nurses and surgeons. Already 300 nurses had responded, the report said.

Fresh troops had moved into Santiago, the newspapers also reported. Here and there trouble still rumbled among the hills. The Cubans weren't sure they wanted the Americans—even for a short time—any more than they had wanted the Spaniards. Troops were needed to maintain order, the papers declared. But, they also demanded, adequate medical care must be provided for the men.

Surgeon General Sternberg already was aware of the need. He had come to the conclusion, from past records, that 15 percent of every unit would be on the sick list. Therefore, the papers announced a few days later, Sternberg had declared that each regiment going to Cuba should be equipped to nurse 15 to 20 patients. Each division should be provided with a hospital of 1,000 beds. He called for a complete staff for these units and petitioned especially for female nurses.

"Why don't they send us?" Clara chafed, as she read the report.

"I've told you several times," Utilie reminded her, "that we're part of the Seventh Corps now, and where the Seventh Corps goes, we go. Where it stays, we stay."

And then orders came. The Seventh Corps was to leave immediately for Santiago de Cuba.■

9

Encounter with the Enemy Postponed

On the seventh day after they left Tampa, Fla., Clara stood at the railing of the transport and stared with fascination. Far off in the distance she glimpsed the green Sierra Maestra mountains, their loftiest peaks wrapped in fluffy, whispy, white clouds. Steep dark ravines cut through the mountains. A mesa appeared to sit at the base of the mountains, and, from that tableand, foothills undulated down until they finally reached ocean level. As the ship drew nearer the shore, distinct objects came into focus. Silhouetted against a cobalt blue sky Clara saw tall cocoanut palms with dropping shaggy fronds, feathery grey-green eucalyptus, and one-sided cedars, misshapen by winds off the seas, their branches pointing shoreward like signs. Perched on the hilltops, antiquated cannons pointed long black noses seaward. Small pink adobe forts and block houses with rifle holes for eyes topped every hill.

A pilot boat pulled up alongside to guide the ship into harbor.

It coasted alongside Morro Castle, sitting astride a jagged, steep cliff that marked the entrance to the harbor. Clara gripped the railing as she peered at the 300-year-old stone castle and caught glimpses of eerie, shadowy tunnels and low-ceilinged, desolate rooms chiseled out of the rock.

The ship moved noiselessly. It altered course slightly. Clara leaned over the rail and strained to see why. Immediately ahead, to one side, weathered timber protruded out of the waters.

"The Merrimac," one of the officers standing next to Clara said. "It sailed in the armada, escaped, was used here first as a warship and then later as a slave ship. Finally the waves pounded it to bits."

Clara heard the ship's engine rumble into reverse gear, and then the vessel came to a shuddering stop. The clattering of heavy chains and the squealing of the winches penetrated the air as the huge iron anchor was dropped. The ship rocked gently. Clara looked. The shore was still a fair distance away. Bobbing around down below were Cubans in small boats. Clara listened with fascination to the Cuban and Spanish dialects as the sun-browned men shouted back and forth to each other.

"Grab your luggage and descend to the boats!" The order echoed over the ship.

Grasping her valise and bedroll, Clara walked unsteadily down the swaying gangplank, handed over her satchel and bedroll first, then, picking up her long skirts in one hand, she grabbed and held on tightly with the other to the hand extended to her from the boat. In she climbed. The boat bobbed like a cork. When every seat on the boat was filled, the men bent and strained under the oars. In a few minutes the bottom of their boat crunched against the sand of the shore. As Clara stepped out, a military officer came forward to greet her.

"All of you nurses will be quartered in town tonight," he said. "Tomorrow you will proceed to the camp at San Luis. I will take you to your quarters."

Clara and he waited for the other nurses and then set off as a group in the horse-drawn carriages. The officer had jumped up and

74

sat down next to Clara in the leading carriage.

"You're lucky coming when you have," he said, giving his whip a gentle flick that sent his horse trotting. "Only two or three months ago you could smell Santiago 10 miles out at sea. No wonder. Piles of mango skins, ashes, and old bones lay everywhere. Filthy rags, dung, garbage, and decaying corpses—ugh! Filth dating back to the 1500s. Open sewers—can you imagine it? Then when the rain came—and it rains here twice a day—it washed all this muck down to the waterfront where that stinking mess piled up knee deep."

Their carriage bumped them around as they sped over the uneven paved street.

"How large is Santiago?" Clara shouted over the noise of the carriage wheels clattering and the horses' hooves echoing off the cobble stones.

"Ordinarily Santiago has 50,000 people. Now it's almost double. Lots of Spanish and American soldiers. We've been mighty lucky that General Wood was put in charge of the city. A man whose energy never seems to burn out. He rises at 5:30 a.m. and drops into bed at midnight, they tell me. People ask him how he can carry on at this pace, day after day, whether he's sick or well. He smiles and says," —they hit a bump and Clara grabbed for her hat—"I have a job to do, and there's a God beyond the rugged hills who gives me power.'"

The officer reined his horse to a walk to reduce the noise.

"Wood said his first job was fourfold: to feed the hungry, to care for the sick, to clean the city, and to bury the dead. He had to do this, he said, to avoid what could be the greatest tragedy of all: a yellow fever epidemic. One day when I was out with him, he pointed with his riding crop with the dog head on it—it's the only weapon he ever carries—to the filth and said, 'It is yellow fever we must fight, and it is going to be a life-and-death struggle. Yellow jack is there,' pointing, 'in that heap of refuse and in that adobe shanty over there, and here under our feet. We've got to fight him with brooms and shovels, with soap and water, and with regulations that will turn this town upside down.' And that's what he's been doing."

The officer reined back his horse. They stopped. He jerked his thumb at an old stone building overgrown with vines.

"That was the Spanish military hospital. Three thousand Spanish soldiers were decaying in there. The stench was so bad it sent bile backing up in your throat. Mud and filth had piled up so many layers deep on the walk about the interior court that you couldn't see whether the walk was paved or not. Infected bloody clothing lay here and there. When we cleaned out the drinking water cistern we found—you won't believe it—human bones, animal bones, old shoes, rags, and, at the bottom, slimy sediment a foot deep."

He clucked his horse, and they moved forward again.

"Red-eyed dogs ran the streets—horrible, mangy creatures, pockmarked with festering sores. They were little more than dried-out hide stretched over bones. We shot the dogs and burned them.

"About this time yellow fever began to rear its head. Somehow it always seems worse in the summer. Understanding how the name alone strikes terror to people, Wood forbade anyone to use the term, though he himself is a doctor. 'Fear can kill,' he said. 'Call it pernicious malaria. People aren't nearly as afraid of malaria.' To isolate the cases, he requisitioned a building for a hospital on an island in the harbor."

"I'd like to see that hospital," Clara said impulsively.

"You would?" The officer looked at her. "Well, if you like, maybe I can take you there this afternoon. But as I was saying, Wood got things under control. The death rate fell from 200 a day to 37."

They were passing now through the downtown section. Clara noticed with amusement the signs: "United States Hotel," "Arizona Saloon," "Chicago Restaurant." Her smile broke into a chuckle when she spotted "Everything is here for sail," "Hot lounches at oll houres" and "Customers treated kindly and quinky." Her chuckles broke into laughter when she spied "Eat here once and you'll never eat elsewhere again."

Her eyes took in an American bank, an American express company, clean streets, gas lamps on poles, and a doctor's office.

"Been told," their guide said, "that white doctors here earn about $6,000 to $8,000 a year. They're really rich bugs."

Leaving the business section, they went rattling down a treelined boulevard.

"It's almost unreal," Clara thought, gazing at the garish colors of the houses: rose, vermilion, canary yellow, robin's egg blue, bilious green, vivid orange. She observed the windows with black iron grating, the red-tiled roofs. Here and there a church steeple pierced the sky. Courtyards, patios, fountains, tiles—her eyes raced to take it all in: goats, donkeys, cats, chickens—and mules and horses pulling two-wheeled carts.

Loud squawking sent her eyes searching the trees. They focused at last on a brilliant parrot, his beady red eyes regarding her suspiciously, his curved beak gaping open to scold her.

Then, unexpectedly, looking incongruous in that setting, they came upon a heap of Mauser rifles.

"They say there are 20,000 in that stack," the officer said.

"The city looks quite clean now," Clara remarked.

"We're getting there," the officer said. "At least we're down to contemporary dirt. To get rid of the filth of the centuries, Wood organized cleaning squads. To begin with, we could find only a dozen wheelbarrows. He sent men to the trenches. They came back with 400 shovels and about two dozen carts. We had to work with what we had. In places we dumped kerosene on streets and set whole streets afire. Wood, in his khaki uniform, rode up and down, supervising." He chuckled. "One of the Rough Riders said that when Wood was through, the flies would starve to death in Santiago."

The officer stopped in front of an old stone building.

"You'll stay here tonight," he said. "Why don't you drop off your bags. Then, if you'd like, I'll take you right now to the hospital for contagious diseases for a short visit."

The visit was disappointing. The aide at the reception desk said that under no circumstances would they allow them inside the wards.

As they were walking down the hall, on the way back to the

carriage, a door suddenly opened. A short, stocky figure bounded out and collided with Clara.

"Beg your pardon!" he exclaimed, backing off.

Clara's guide smiled in recognition.

"Dr. Agramonte, this is Miss Clara Maass, contract nurse with the Seventh Army Corps."

Intense brown eyes looked into curious blue ones.

"Miss Maass, this is Dr. Aristides Agramonte, bacteriologist, doing research on yellow fever patients."

"On what remains of those who didn't make it rather," Dr. Agramonte corrected.

"He's younger than he looks," Clara thought. "If he shaved off that ponderous mustache and that neatly cropped beard of his, we'd know how old he really is."

A worker passed, and Dr. Agramonte exchanged a few words in Spanish with him.

Then, addressing Clara, "Where are you from?"

"East Orange, New Jersey."

"Really? I received my education at Columbia and was working for the Health Department of New York when I volunteered. Was born in Cuba though. Dad was a doctor here. This is really home for me. You going to be here long?"

"I don't know."

"Miss Maass probably will be at the camp at San Luis first. I'll be taking her there tomorrow," the officer said.

The brooding brown eyes examined Clara carefully. "Are you tough? Though I don't know which is worse, that mudhole or this furnace of yellow fever. They send all their yellow fever patients to us for isolation." A pause, then, "I wish you well. Good day, Miss Maass."

Dr. Agramonte bowed slightly, then opened the door and went back to his cadavers and his microscope.

"One of our most brilliant bacteriologists," the officer said. "And determined to lick yellow fever."

Clara felt a little shiver skitter down her back, and goose pimples popped out on her arms.

"We have very little yellow fever at San Luis, the military camp, 26 miles from here. The few cases that pop up we shoot off here to Santiago in order to isolate them. Have enough troubles of our own at the camp without yellow fever. Malaria. Typhoid. The camp's full of it."

As they were about to leave the hospital a middle-aged, dark-skinned man arrived. He greeted Clara's guide. Clara's guide acknowledged the greeting, then, touching Clara's arm, he said. "Dr. Guiteras, I'd like you to meet this contract nurse, newly arrived. Miss Clara Maass from New Jersey."

Dr. Juan Guiteras briefly removed his stiff broad-brimmed straw hat. "Please to meet you," he murmured, then hastened on his way to the hospital.

"Dr. Juan Guiteras," Clara's guide explained. "Another Cuban. Studied at—the University of Pennsylvania I think it was. Sharp fellow. Like Agramonte. Has a real crusade going to end yellow fever. Says a person isn't immune to yellow jack just because you've been born where there's lots of it, but admits he still doesn't know what causes it."

Outside the hospital the officer said, "Perhaps I should take you back to your quarters now. You'll want to freshen up and get something to eat. Tomorrow'll be a long day."

The next morning early they set off on horseback for Camp San Luis. On the outskirts of town they came upon small houses, made of mud plastered over pole frames, with roofs of thatch from palm trees or bark from cocoanut trees. Clara saw women in gaily colored clothes, men with sombreros, and barefoot children. The children ran up to them and began to swear in English. The officer's neck reddened.

"Do they know what they're saying?" asked Clara.

The officer lifted his cap and readjusted it on his head. "Probably not," he replied. "They pick up things fast."

Suddenly an urchin with toothpick legs let out a screeching whistle that faintly resembled a bugle call. It sent Clara's horse careening and neighing in alarm.

"Easy there," the officer soothed, reaching across to steady the horse.

The boys hugged their middles and slapped their thighs and laughed uproariously.

Then another ragged one approached Clara and danced alongside her horse. Pointing at Clara's black, high-button shoes, he began to chant, "Shine? Shine 'em up?" An unmistakable New York accent accompanied the chant.

Clara laughed. "No time for a shine today," she said.

The officer grinned. "General Wood has really won the hearts of the children. One day he threw a grand party for them. Took them for a ride around the harbor on government ships. Had bands on board playing for them and military aides ladling out lemonade from barrels. It was quite a day."

They rode on, leaving the children behind.

"Santiago province is almost like a little world in itself," the officer explained. "It takes five days by steamer to go from here to Havana. This country here is all privately folded away in the mountains, sprinkled here and there with a few sparsely populated plains. But the hinterland mostly is a hideout for robbers and brigands. General Wood says the country reminds him of New Mexico. I ain't never been there, so I don't know."

"You mean," asked Clara, "that you can't go from here by road to Havana?"

"Nope. Maybe 'way back there once was a road, but all that's left now is a broken bridge here and there and a crushed culvert."

They rode on in silence.

"Look up there, ahead, Miss," the officer said after a while. "That there is San Juan hill. That's where Teddy Roosevelt's 'Rough Riders' grappled with the Spaniards."

They climbed the hill slowly, weaving around bushes and shrubs. Skeletons of horses, their ribbed cages broken but still recognizable, gave mute testimony to the life-and-death struggle that had taken place.

Passing over the hill they found themselves on rough terrain, crisscrossed with rivers and creeks and cluttered with shrubs and boulders. It had begun to rain. The rain steamed up Clara's glasses and trickled off her chin. The officer lifted his felt hat carefully and tipped off the water that had gathered on the brim.

"Let's stop here for a minute, Miss," he said. "Follow me."

He led the way to a place where they could look down into a ravine. A small river ran sluggishly down the gully, getting trapped here and there in small, green, stagnant pools overgrown with tropical vines. Involuntarily Clara put her hand over her nose.

"Look, there to the right, halfway down. You'll see what you're smelling."

Clara wiped her glasses, then, leaning forward and squinting, she saw half-submerged in the pool the rotting remains of a mule. She turned away.

"Are the soldiers drinking this water? No wonder they've dysentery. And what a hotbed for malarial mosquitoes!" she cried.

They mounted their horses and continued on the way, passing a herd of mules.

"Without mules we'd never have gotten supplies to our troops. The wagons they tried to use first sank in the mud. Must be about 200 mules over there. . . . Talking about mules—when the Spaniards withdrew, know what they did? They took mule manure and threw it into all the wells. We've had an awful time cleaning them out."

"As I said yesterday, you're lucky, Miss, that you've come now instead of right after the fighting ended." He tipped the rain off his hat again. "That ocean pounds the shores so hard down where our troops disembarked, some of the barges jes' sunk right to the bottom. And some of the transports bounced around and collided with each other until they were almost finished. They couldn't land the supplies. Didn't have proper landing gear for shores like these. The horses. They had horses on board. Tried to land them. Held their heads and tried to show them the shore. Then pushed them in. Some made it, but many didn't. Got water in their ears and got all confused. Swam in circles. Or took off for open sea. Or tried to clamber back on board the ship and got chewed up by the propellers." The officer sighed. "Such beauties some of them were too."

"And then this hilly ground. They couldn't use wagons to get the supples from the ship to the troops. Had hospital equipment on the ship but couldn't get it to the men. The first surgical tents had no sides, just canvas stretched over poles. They carried the wounded in on stretchers and placed them on tables. The surgeons, some of them stripped naked to the waist, examined their wounds, all through the day and on into the night, using only candle light. For 21 consecutive hours that one day they stood. No sleep. Little rest or food. The great bloody wave of injured men kept rolling back from the battle line. Thought it would never stop. The tents for wounded soldiers overflowed, so all the litter squad could do was carry the wounded men and lay them, often half-naked, on the rain-sodden ground under the stars. Many of them were weak and trembling from encounters with the surgeon's knife also, yet they had no choice but to lie in the high wet grass with no one to nurse them, no one to wet their lips with water or comfort them."

Clara's guide reined back his horse, dismounted, pulled off his shoe, then his sock, and searched his sock till he found a bramble, which he pulled out.

"Been feeling that thing the last hour," he explained, mounting his horse again. "Let's see, where was I? Oh, yes, we were without tents. Well, we got so desperate we sent word to Miss Clara Barton. She responded immediately with blankets, clothing, cornmeal gruel, milk, beef broth, and coffee.

"But the rain poured on. July 11 will always be known as 'the night it rained.' Raging streams ran all around. Streaks of lightning ripped open the sky and lit up those mountain ranges so clear you couldn't believe it. Then a stunning clap-crash-bang of thunder would send all of us shaking. Thought for sure the end of the world had come. Even Teddy Roosevelt's tent blew over. He ran to the kitchen tent where the cook wrapped him up in a blanket and put him to bed on a table.

"Finally, tents arrived. It was great to see the wounded men off the ground, onto cots, and into tents. All those who had had abdominal surgery died, so the surgeons stopped performing those operations.

"Then the sickness began. The sickness was worse 'n any wounds the men had. Some were so weak they couldn't even use the buckets by the sides of their cots.

"The men burned with fever, and there wasn't any decent water to drink and no kettles to boil water in. We ran out of Red Cross supplies and were stuck with hardtack and green, unroasted coffee beans. Ever tried to make coffee out of green beans?" He shook his head. "And no stoves. The men tried to cook in their mess kits over open fires. Well, it was really bad for a while, but the men were brave. Then ships with food began to come. But that brought disappointment too. The canned beef was terrible. At least most people said so, though General Wood kept saying it was delicious. But Clara Barton. She showed up at camp again one day. All dressed up in a long dark skirt and a white blouse, her dark hair all piled up in curls on top of her head, real purty. She asked to taste some of the beef stew, and was she mad! 'Sinew, bones, and skin!' she raged. 'This stuff is what's left after they've squeezed all the juice from beef for bouillon.' I heard she went back home and really raised a ruckus.

"And the potatoes. They had gone rotten in the hold on the way over. The smell! If the devil himself had been around, I'm sure he couldn't have stood it.

"It won't be much farther now, Miss," he said, noticing Clara shifting in her saddle. "And the flour," he continued, "I'll bet the flour was packed for the soldiers of the Civil War. Bread made out of flour full of small white worms, beans full of weevils—and the hominy? Musty." He sighed. "We all got so all we could think about was food—good food. We'd lie and imagine what we'd have if we could. Real steaks. Potatoes. Gravy. And pie. Apple pie. With ice cream. And real coffee, with sugar and cream.

"Anyway," he said, reaching over to scratch his horse behind the ears, "things got better after a while. We got some decent food and some stoves to cook it on. And after the surrender the ships brought 65 doctors, I heard tell, and 129 nurses, many of them women. Still a few left here. 'Course not all were trained as I understand you're trained.

"At first we didn't know what we was going to do with the women in this hole. But then after a while we didn't know what we would do without them." He laughed. "The women really got things organized. When the fighting was going on, it was a mess. Not enough doctors. Not enough tents. No trained people to take care of the sick. Tried to train some of the volunteers, but you can guess how that went. Yes'm, those trained nurses sure put things right." He struck the open palm of his left hand with his fist as though to emphasize the point.

They had reached the camp. Clara stared at the field peppered with tents.

"We're real proud of the organization we have now," the officer said again. "Come in and meet some of the boys in the hospital tents. They'll be glad to see a woman, even if they're sicker than a dog."

The officer held the canvas flap to one side and Clara stepped inside. She found herself looking down two long rows of cots.

"Must be at least 50 on each side," she thought. As she reached down to straighten the blanket of the first cot, she was dismayed at the clamminess of the wool.

"Here's another nurse come to care for you fellows," the officer announced.

"You look as though you're having a miserable time," Clara said to the young lad under the blanket.

The boy stared at her. "You goin' be stationed here? A young woman like you?"—then, "God save your soul!"

Clara laughed lightly.

"You'll be feeling better in a few days. . . . On the way up I saw fruit: oranges, bananas, pineapple, mangoes, papaya. Do you get fruit to eat?"

"We're gettin' some now, Miss." An older man from another cot spoke up. "Trouble is, when we haven't had it for a while we eat too much of it. It's all the fresh fruit we eat, I sez, that brings on the fever."

84

From yet another bed a young soldier raised himself on his elbow. "Ah," he exclaimed, "when that dreaded fever sails in on you," his eyes rolled, "sad is the day. That monster regards neither black nor white. Today you feel ill. Tomorrow," he sucked in his cheeks, "your sunken cheeks, thin hands," he spread out his own scrawny hands with their long, dirty fingernails, "and weak system all say that the bone yard will claim another victim and retire a soul from suffering."

"I know," another called out, "and I don't want to die here. When a person dies here he is buried in a pine box, with two or three underneath him or on top of him."

"Humph!" chimed in another. "Someone told me they rent coffins for the funeral service, but after it's all over, they open the coffin and dump the corpse into the grave. Then the coffin is ready for the next occupant. Me neither—I don't want to die here."

"Who says you're going to die here?" A bright-faced middle-aged man who had entered the tent spoke. "Things aren't as they were at the first when the troops came back from the fighting all worn out. It was bad then. But those men were worn out from fighting. You'll pull out of this real fast."

"At least," one of the younger boys said, "we didn't have to lie in the trenches with the rain pouring in hour after hour. At first I felt kinda angry that we weren't getting in on the combat. But after I heard some of the stories—well, I began to think I was just plain lucky.

"When those yellow-skinned, scrawny troops were leaving, all glassy-eyed and wiggly-walking and hardly able to get on the transport, one guy got ahold of me and said, 'Man! you ain't seen nuthin'. You should've been with me in that old Spanish prison they threw me into when I was wounded. There I was lying, surrounded by all those beheading blocks, all covered with human hair and dried on blood. And pieces of rope danging from the rafters overhead, from which many a Cuban had been hung. Old bloody blankets in the corner."

"What do you do on your days off, when you're well and back

in the camp?" Clara asked, determined to steer the conversation to more pleasant subjects.

"Days off!" snorted one. "We go down to the river and wash and put on clean clothes. Then we go to a Cuban home, and the family comes out, and we sit in a circle. But it is no use, for we cannot talk with each other. We can only smile or sigh and make motions and then sit silent again."

They had come to the end of the long row of beds. The bright-faced, middle-aged man, who had accompanied them took Clara by the elbow and guided her out.

"The situation isn't all bad," he assured her. "In my spare time I've been holding preaching services and conducting Bible classes. Next Sunday I hope to baptize about a hundred in one of these creeks." He paused.

"Things sure are a sight better than it was right after the fighting. I got to talk with some of the fellows of the Fifth Corps just before they left. So many were dying of fever every day they said that they couldn't dig graves fast enough. So they took to cremating the bodies. But then the rain put out the cremation fires. They had to stop blowing the bugles and shooting off the rifle volleys when someone died, because it got too depressing for the men in the tents to hear the guns go off so often." He shook his head. "But we've still got plenty of misery in those tents, Miss. And plenty outside in the countryside too."

Even as he spoke, a gaunt man shuffled up, his brown face looking like a walnut. His belly popped out above his loin cloth.

"Me comida," he begged. ("Feed me.")

Clara's guide broke into Spanish. "That tent over there? See it? Go there. They'll give you something to eat." Then, turning to Clara again, "General Wood has been doing all he can. Heard that last week alone they handed out 35,000 rations. We need medicine for these poor folks too, but all we have is quinine. But it's been heartbreaking. One day I saw little kids trying to wake up a mother who wouldn't wake up. Never. She was stone dead." A sigh escaped. "It's not a pretty situation, Miss. Sure you can handle it?"

"I'll try," Clara said, "I'll try my hardest."

In her own tent that night Clara turned restlessly on her camp cot. "It's all so different," she thought. "Our German Hospital seems thousands of miles away and belonging to a different age. It's different from Florida and Georgia too. And this country. I feel as though I've stepped back 500 years in time." Finally, exhausted from all she had seen and heard that day, Clara feel asleep.

Clara awakened to find two sentries standing guard outside her tent.

"You'll need them," one of the doctors declared, when she asked him about it. "We've got a lot of volunteers in this camp. Had quite a time with them when they first came. Disorderly. Insubordinate. General Wood himself had to move in and take over for a while. They've settled down considerably now, but some of them, cut off from their own women, don't know how to behave properly when they see a woman." He paused and winked. "Especially a pretty young one like you."

The days that followed were full to the brim for Clara as she gave what nursing care she could. She listened to complaints. She calmed nervous fears and assured the men they would recover. Her cheerful attitude and irrepressible confidence quieted the restless men better than any bromide. Miraculously, most of them recovered.

As she moved among the men, she heard one doctor referred to often. Dr. Gorgas.

"What a saint!" said many a soldier who had recovered and was assisting in the hospital. "His kindly face poured healing into us. His soft words of concern were like butter."

"And when he smiled," another said, "it made a person feel better all over."

"I never met a man," a serious-faced, scarred older man said slowly, "who knew so well how to keep hope alive in a fellow."

"Why isn't he here now?" Clara asked.

"Poor fellow! Haven't you heard? Malaria got him too. Really flattened him. He just couldn't get going again. When he finally got out of bed, he would weave around like a drunk man, eyes all glassy. They sent him home to recover. God bless his soul."

Two events lightened the weeks both for Clara and the men. One was a Thanksgiving celebration. General Wood had felt it only proper to pause and thank God for all that had been accomplished. The city was reasonably clean. The general health of the populace was greatly improved. In September, appalled that only 60 percent of the white and 80 percent of the colored population could read or write, Wood had gathered 4,000 children in schools. He also opened a school for women. Streets were being paved. Wood put an end to bullfighting and public gambling. He had prosecuted bakers and marketmen for falsification of weights and scales. He had ceased to give free handouts to those who wouldn't work. The morale of the people was good. In every way Santiago was experiencing new life. "Surely we must thank God and acknowledge that without His help we could no have done this," Wood said.

Clara and the other nurses giggled, however, when the report drifted back to them as to how some of the young officers had wound up their Thanksgiving celebrations. Their superior, Wood, had forbidden gambling for money in the city. So the young fellows took refuge on a ship anchored in harbor. They played poker, not for money, but for clothes. As dawn began to awaken the city, young men with newspapers wrapped around them climbed into little boats to go ashore. Somehow Wood heard of it. He ordered his police to look the other way if they saw any young men in newsprint furtively stealing their way home.

The other break came early in December when the whole populace rejoiced with Wood when he was promoted to major general. The people rang church bells. They toasted him in their cafes. They sang and danced. It was a magnificent tribute to a man who had been stubbornly resisted and rebelled against when he first assumed command of the city. The joyous spirit of celebration infiltrated the hospital too, and when Clara made rounds that night, the men talked about how much better they felt.

"There's no medicine on earth like joy, success, and good news," Clara remarked to her tentmate that night as she fell wearily, but contentedly, onto her cot.

And then in February 1899, after many weeks spent nursing in the hospital tents, Clara's letter of honorable discharge came. Her unit, little by little, was to be sent back to the States. By May 3, 1899, the transfer was to be completed and the corps disbanded.

As she stood at the railing of the ship watching the palm and eucalyptus shores of Santiago fade out of sight, Clara sighed. For some reason she felt a sense of infinite loss.

But Clara was to return, and her return visit would introduce her firsthand to the deadly yellow killer. But before that encounter, yet another adventure lay ahead for her.■

TOP: Clara Maass' orders from the Surgeon General of U.S. to report for duty as a "contract nurse" in Manila; TOP RIGHT: Dr. Carroll, Yellow Fever Researchist; CENTER: The burning of the village of Siboney; BOTTOM LEFT: Dr. Walter Reed, Yellow Fever Researchist; BOTTOM RIGHT: Clara Maass' contract for nursing services in Jacksonville, Florida.

10

Yellow Jack Attacks

Back home in East Orange with her mother, Clara at first welcomed the opportunity to rest. But as the weeks passed she grew fidgety. The small talk of the townspeople about weather and neighbors stifled her. She longed to be back with the troops. Her news-hungry eyes plucked from the newspapers accounts of the unrest in the Philippines. People were rioting, she read, because although the United States had promised Cuba the opportunity to set up self-government, President McKinley believed the people of the Philippines were not ready for it. American policy, he tried to explain, should be "not to exploit, but to develop, civilize, educate, and train the Filipinos in the science of self-government."

But General Emilio Aguinaldo, who had called together 12,000 revolutionaries and fought alongside the Americans in freeing Manila from the Spanish, resented this policy. In protest he was leading the insurrectionists in agitation for self-government, and, the newspapers said, it looked likely that the president would be sending more troops to Manila to keep everything under control.

Clara reread the last paragraph, and then sat down and wrote a letter to Dr. Anita McGee. Dr. McGee's reply prompted Clara to write another letter, this one addressed to the Surgeon General, George Sternberg.

Brigadier General Sternberg, Clara had learned, was considered one of the most conscientious and progressive surgeon generals the country had ever had. Many put him as a scientist in the same category as Koch, Pasteur, Lister, and Metchnikoff, all of whom knew Sternberg and spoke appreciatively of him. But even more. Sternberg was a deeply devout man, a Lutheran by confession, and motivated by compassion for all who suffered. It was said of him that he sought to comfort personally the bereaved families of all soldiers who fell in battle. This concern manifested itself in the lavish and extensive provisions he made to care for wounded and sick soldiers. If he is sending other nurses and doctors to the Philippines, why shouldn't he send me too? Clara reasoned. So Nov. 8, 1899, she wrote this letter:

> I have the honor respectfully to request that my name be placed on the list of nurses sailing to Manila, P. I., from New York, and that I be sent on the first transport leaving. Having served as contract nurse in the field hospitals of the Seventh Army Corps continuously and with satisfaction from October 1, 1898, to February 5, 1899, I have been notified by Dr. McGee that I am eligible for service in the Philippines, and it is my desire to be sent there, as I prefer a tropical climate to that of New York. I am in excellent health and I have a good constitution and am accustomed to the hardships of field service.

Clara mailed the letter and then settled down again to wait for an answer.

Nov. 20 a knock summoned her to the door. A blue-uniformed boy handed her a telegram. Eagerly Clara took it, ripped it open and read: "In accordance with telegraphic order from the Surgeon General, U.S. Army, dated Nov. 18, 1899, Miss Clara L. Maass, Contract Nurse, will proceed to Manila on the Army transport Logan and report to the Chief Surgeon for duty." It was signed by the Medical Superintendent of the U. S. Army Transport Service.

The <u>Logan.</u> When was it due to leave? Clara put through a telephone call and gasped. As she put the receiver back on the hook, her hand shook.

"Mother," her voice was almost a whisper, "I've only two <u>hours</u> to get to the <u>Logan</u> in New York."

She dashed to her bedroom and yanked down her suitcase. "Call a cab so I can get to the railroad station," she called to her sister.

Hurriedly she snatched clothes from her drawers and closet and crammed them into her bag.

"Don't forget your telegram, Dear." Clara's mother's hands trembled as she thrust the telegram into Clara's hands. "You'll need it, won't you, to get on the ship? What dress are you going to wear, Dear?"

"No time to change clothes. I'll have to go as I am. My Bible. Where's my Bible? Can't go without my Bible. Where are the babies, so I can kiss them good-bye?" She reached down and gathered three-year old Elsie into her arms. "'Bye, Elsie, Honey!" She rubbed her face in her small sister's soft hair. She straightened and went over to the cradle where baby Arthur lay sleeping. She stood looking at him, ran her forefinger down his soft cheek, bent over and whispered, "'Bye, Baby Arthur!" Then turning to her mother and wrapping her arms around her, "Say good-bye to Papa." She kissed her mother. "'Bye, Mother dear! Don't worry. I'll write." And she was out the door.

A train ride to Hoboken. Then onto the ferry to cross the North River. It moved so slowly! Clara longed to be able to get behind it and push. She was the first one off. Leaning sideways against the weight of her heavy suitcase, she ran up the incline to the cabstand on Barclay Street.

"Quick," she panted to the driver of the hansom cab she jumped into. "The main pier, as fast as you can go. I have a ship to catch."

Through the streets they tore, the driver whipping his horse

and shouting and yelling for others to get out of the way. Ahh—
there was the <u>Logan,</u> still at the dock. Visitors were leaving. Clara
grabbed her bag and ran up the gangplank. On deck she collapsed
on a wooden slat bench. She had made it! "Manila, here I come!" she
said to herself, feeling excitement mount at this new adventure
before her.

The sense of excitement paled as the ship steamed slowly on
its way, day after day, around Cape Horn and across the Pacific.
The transport was crowded, the seas rough. Boys who were
quartered in the holds on hammocks would come crawling up on
the decks for air. Many were so ill they would crawl on all fours over
to the rail to lean over and be sick. They complained about the
nauseating odors below and begged to be allowed to stay on deck.

Clara found herself with some other nurses in a section of the
ship that had a porthole opening to the seas. Their bunks,
unyielding with wooden slats, were 36 inches wide. Four bunks up
and down didn't allow space to sit up in between. The aisle
between the bunks was so narrow that the ladies drew numbers
and took turns getting dressed and undressed. But electric lights
and a fan brought light and comfort. A soldier on watch, with a rifle
across his knees, sat in the corridor immediately outside their door.

One section of the ship quartered live beef animals to be
slaughtered for the troops on arrival. Days when the wind blew
from that direction the passengers were reminded of the presence
of the cattle. Sometimes at night their restless mooing awakened
Clara.

The weather improved and rewarded them with calm blue-
green seas. Evenings the nurses sat out on the open deck, their
backs against the wall of the cabins. They watched the moonlight
shimmer and sparkle and dance and gleam across the rippling
waters. At night, back in their cabin, the creaking of the ship, the
lapping of the waves, and the gentle rocking of the ship lulled them
to sleep. Even so they were glad to learn their journey soon would
be over.

Everyone was on deck the day the <u>Logan</u> steamed past the
lighthouse with the huge stone fortress behind it and on into Manila

harbor. Before them sprawled the city of Manila, founded in 1571, now with a population of 300,000. Pink adobe forts and block houses of Spanish design surrounded the city. Catholic church buildings pierced the skyline.

The Pasig River divided the city. On the south bank of the Pasig, surrounded on three sides by the river and the bay, lay the "Old City," a massive stone fortress built in the 18th century. To the north, newer suburbs sprawled out.

The streets, Clara discovered, were narrow, but the center of the new city was as busy as Newark's downtown area. Street car tracks ran down the streets. Rickshaws pulled by small horses squeezed by. Buildings were three or four stories high, all with awnings or drop shades to ward off the hot rays of the sun. The men in the city, Clara noted, wore spotless white suits, black ties, black shoes. All wore some type of hat: derbies, straw hats with broad brims, or cork-lined sun helmets. The women strolled along hatless, their long black hair falling loose down their backs. There appeared to be as many women in business as men.

In the quarters to which she had been brought for the night Clara relaxed. She watched the sun slowly lower itself into the waters. The coolness of the night air stroked her cheeks. Gulls swept in from the ocean and darted in and out the bell towers of the cathedrals, scaring out hordes of bats that flew out, their wings whirring softly as they dipped and darted. As Clara watched, the lights of the city and the lights of the ships in harbor twinkled on. The whole atmosphere was one of peace. The only dissonant sound was the boom of cannons. "Wonder why they're shooting cannon?" Clara thought and then fell asleep.

Roosters crowed her awake the next morning. She heard the mellow pealing of bells, calling the people to mass. Outside her window the wooden shoes of the bread man echoed on the pavement. She heard the swish of the broom man sweeping the walks. A horse clopped past on the cobble street. The snap of the driver's whip speeded up the clopping, and the carriage wheels creaked in protest as they rolled faster.

It was the last morning Clara would be conscious of sounds of normal, contented living in Manila. For the Field Reserve Hospital to which she was assigned was crowded with long rows of very sick men. Typhoid, pneumonia, malaria, dengue fever, typhus—all the enemies of safe living in the tropics had lined up to attack the nonimmune intruders. The peaceful atmosphere Clara had basked in the first night was deceptive, she realized. For yellow fever, the most awesome killer ravaging the world at that time, mysteriously had made its appearance too, and superstition and fear gripped the city. People tried every means they could think of to keep the fever away. They smoked tobacco until they became ill. They dipped sponges in vinegar and tied them over their mouths. They ate enormous amounts of garlic until no one could come near them. They dipped ropes in tar and wore them around their waists. They lit bonfires, and, Clara learned, shot off cannons to clear the air.

"Yellow jack" some called the fever, referring to the navy quarantine flag that flew over buildings where victims were rotting with it. "El vomito negro" the Spaniards had called it, referring to the black vomit that resulted from blood, altered by stomach acids, ejected from the stomach. The blood came from broken vessels in the walls of the stomach.

Day after day as Clara moved among the sick, the book she had read about the yellow fever epidemic of 1878 came alive. Now with her own eyes she could trace the course of the disease and see it ravage her patients. Although struggling with the helpless feeling of having come to grips with a giant infinitely stronger than she, still she nursed on. She applied cold cloths to perspiring foreheads, wrapped her patients in wet sheets to bring down their raging fevers, and held them in bed when they became hysterical. Always she talked with the men, soothed and cheered them, assured them they would survive, and talked them into believing it.

Days grew into weeks, and weeks into months—seven months in all, far into 1900. Still she carried on faithfully, thinking always of the sick men, disregarding herself. Some nights when weariness would plunge her into depression, she would sob into her pillow when she returned to her tent. When her crying ceased, she would pray: for the tortured, limp men in the tents, for the

96

unutterably weary nurses and doctors, for her worried family back home, and for strength for herself. Always, and above all, she would pray fervently that someone would discover what caused yellow fever, so that it could be prevented. Sometimes as she prayed, anger at this disease that could destroy the lives of healthy men and cause them to become almost unmanageable maniacs would flare up. But the next morning when she arose from her cot, her anger had burned out. It had left instead a residue of steellike determination to fight back at the disease. With compassion pooled in her eyes, but with resolution reflected in the firm set of her small chin, she would go back to her men to sing hope into their despairing hearts and rekindle in their eyes the determination to live.

Then came the morning when the depression was too heavy to throw off. Indescribable weariness wrapped arms around her like a giant octopus. She struggled feebly to get up, then sank back on her cot.

"I'm not feeling well this morning," she said to her roommate. "I think I've caught cold."

Her roommate glanced at Clara's flushed cheeks. Muffling anxiety she said, "You better rest. You've been going at it awfully hard for months now."

The next day Clara was whimpering softly. "I ache all over," she complained. "It feels as though every bone in my body is breaking."

The next day the fever was gone, and aside from extreme weariness Clara felt better. The following day her temperature soared again.

"Oh, my head," she moaned. "It's like a boil. I can't bear to move it. It aches so terribly behind my eyes. My bones! Take the blankets off. I can't stand them on me." Tears trickled down her cheeks.

Clara's roommate said nothing but disappeared, only to reappear a few minutes later with a doctor.

"Dengue fever," the doctor said, after checking over Clara.

"The natives here call it 'break-bone fever.' You'll be over the worst of it in a week's time."

Then, tweaking the bump under the blanket where her big toe was, "You can be glad it wasn't yellow fever."

But dengue fever, though usually not fatal, this time threatened Clara's life. Her frail body, overworked for so many months, was unable to fight back against the disease. Anxiously the doctors and nurses hovered over Clara. At last she rallied, but as the days passed her tired body still could not respond with enough strength so she could leave her bed.

"Why can't I get well?" she cried to her doctor one day.

"Clara," he said gently, "we're going to send you home. You need a long rest away from all the heartaches of this place. We'll reserve a bunk for you on the first ship sailing for the U. S." He patted her arm. "We're glad it wasn't yellow fever. Be thankful for that and be glad you can go home."■

11

Hot on the Trail of Yellow Jack

Three months later, refreshed and in vibrant health, Clara was visiting her friends at Trefz Hall.

Where are you off to next?" one of the girls asked.

"Cuba!" Clara's eyes sparkled. "I just received the telegram today. It said, 'Come at once,' and was signed, 'Gorgas, Chief Sanitary Officer.' I read a call he had sent out for nurses. I wrote him and said I was willing to come. Gorgas!" Her voice betrayed her excitement. "When I was nursing in Santiago, Gorgas was a legendary doctor among the troops. Everyone loved him. And now I'm going to get a chance to work under him. I can hardly wait."

"But the war is over."

"One war is over," Clara corrected. "They're still fighting the battle against yellow jack. The Secretary of War has appointed a Yellow Fever Commission to track down the villain. I'm off to nurse yellow fever patients, and, in doing so, I hope to observe the investigations first hand."

"Aren't you afraid of getting yellow fever?"

Clara shrugged. "I didn't get it all the time I was in Manila. I was surrounded by it there." She laughed and went on. "I've other news too, only it's really a secret. I haven't told even my family about this yet."

The girls crowded around.

"When I get back from Cuba," she paused and then added dramatically, "I'm going to get married."

"Clara! To whom? When did this happen? Where?"

Clara laughed. "I call him 'my Captain,'" she said. "There! that's all I'm going to tell you. You'll have to wait for more when I get back."

No amount of teasing or begging would shake Clara from her resolve. "I can have a secret if I want to, can't I?" was her only response.

Another short ocean voyage faced Clara. A few days later she disembarked from her ship to gaze with wonder at a sparkling clean city. Havana had just emerged, sputtering and protesting, from a gigantic enounter with soapsuds, cleanser, disinfectants, carbolic acid, and scrub brushes. Major William Crawford Gorgas, Chief Sanitary Officer, was determined to close in upon and conquer his enemy of a lifetime: yellow fever. He fervently believed the fever could be scrubbed and disinfected out of existence. General Sternberg, it was rumored, shared the same conviction.

Clara hailed a horse-drawn hansom cab.

"To the hospital," she directed.

"Which one, Miss?" the driver asked, holding his whip aloft in readiness. "The Military Hospital here in town? Or the Columbia Barracks Hospital eight miles out of town? Fourteen hundred troops garrisoned there. You wouldn't be going there. Or Dependientes or Covadonga or Benefica? Or the Civilian Hospital, Las Animas?"

"That's it!" Clara interrupted. "Las Animas."

The driver nodded. "Should have guessed. Las Animas has mostly American doctors and nurses. Folks who've been there say it's just like an American hospital." He glanced at Clara. "You going to nurse yellow fever patients?"

"I guess."

"They bring all the really sick ones to Las Animas, you know."

"No, I didn't know."

"Yup! Send their ambulance to pick them up from all over town. Carry them in on stretchers and send them out walking."

"Really?" A note of joy.

"Most of the time. Only about one out of five don't make it, they tell me. They 'spect they'll total up 'most 300 cases this year, I've heard. That hospital has the best reputation in town for helping people get well. Dr. Havard—he's the big chief surgeon of the U. S. Army forces in Cuba—Dr. Havard says it's mostly because of the good nursing care that trained lady nurses like you give. We owe a lot to folks like you, Ma'am." The driver raised his straw hat.

"I'm glad I could come," Clara said.

They clattered on over the brick pavement. Clara stared with interest at the many two-wheeled carts, carrying farm produce, pulled by horses, donkeys, or sturdy oxen. Lighter-weight four-wheeled carriages like the one she was in rattled past, toting passengers. A track ran down the center of the street, and at the far end Clara saw a trolley car being pulled by three horses—a lead horse followed by two. Everywhere two-and three-story brick and concrete buildings crowded out to the streets. Arched colonnades and doorways, balconies with grillwork, and roof overhangs elaborately carved gave a Spanish touch to the city. Men and women strolled the streets, the men wearing loosely fitting pants, coats, and wide-brimmed hats, the women long full-skirted dresses or skirts and blouses. All seemed to be carrying loads wrapped in bright cloth bundles and huge black umbrellas, to shield them from the hot sun, Clara guessed.

They passed through the main section of the city and headed for the outskirts. The road began to wind and climb gently.

"Las Animas Hospital is situated on a right pretty spot," the driver said. "The hospital got its name from the hill it sits on. We'll climb a good 50 feet. Nice view of the city from up there. And room to stretch too. The hospital sprawls over about 12 or 15 acres, I'd guess. That's a lot nicer than the congestion we've got in the city. So many foreigners have come the last little while that we're scrunched in, about 9 or 10 people to every 2 or 3 rooms. Ain't comfortable being so crowded." The driver slowed down his horse as they negotiated another curve and continued to climb.

"The Spaniards used the hospital buildings as barracks for a battalion of their top engineers," he went on. "But when the Americans came, they appropriated it as a military hospital first but then transferred it to the city authorities. They spent over $20,000 making it into a first-class hospital, I've been told. Folks say as how you can get as good nursing care and food and have as good surroundings as you would in the best hospital in New York. Of course I say," and the driver smiled at Clara, "that our natural surroundings are a sight prettier than New York."

They rounded the last curve, and their horse trotted up the semicircular drive leading to the front of the hospital. Clara's eyes swept over the one-story high, smoothly stuccoed and newly painted building with red-tiled roof and arched doorways. Concrete sidewalks led to several smaller separate buildings. Green shrubs and flowering trees enhanced the setting of the chalk-white buildings.

"It is pretty," Clara exlaimed.

The driver helped her dismount. She walked up to the arched door and rang the bell.

An aide appeared. Clara introduced herself. The aide bowed. Yes, Dr. Gorgas was expecting her. He had left word that she should be taken to the nurses' quarters.

That evening, visiting with the other nurses, Clara commented on the surgical cleanliness of the city.

"I think I even smelled carbolic acid and lime," she remarked.

The nurses chortled.

"Probably," Nellie Lewis said. "You should have seen Havana a year ago. When Dr. Gorgas arrived, this city had to be one of the filthiest cities in the world. Bloated corpses rotted in the gutters, alongside dead mules and horses. The smell—ugh! Hordes of huge blue-black flies hovered over the city in clouds—and I mean clouds. Their buzzing zinged in all day long. The war had disrupted whatever street-cleaning system they had before, and the flies were having a heyday. When we walked outside we either had to talk with our hands cupped over our mouths or talk through clenched teeth. Otherwise some flies would be sure to soar right in. I accidentally swallowed some to begin with." She shook her body and her head. "Those flies. They planted their hairy feet in the pus that oozed from the eyes and around the nose and mouths of the starving children and sat and gorged on the yellow mucus. The children were too lethargic to chase them off, or else they figured it wasn't worth trying, for as quickly as the flies were swatted away, they'd return."

"It really was awful," Miss Olbrian, the head nurse, comfirmed. "Garbage piled up, drains clogged and backed up, sewers overflowed. Rats," she shuddered, "—they actually ran around in the day time and gnawed on the corpses. Vultures circled overhead, then dropped down and pecked away. They always went for the eyes first. Unbelievable." She shuddered. "Then there were the land crabs that crawled all over the corpses and devoured them. I remember walking past a corpse one day and staring with horror. The crab stopped its gnawing, raised its head, and its beady eyes seemed to ask me what I was doing disturbing it." She covered her eyes with her hands, as though to shut out the memory. After a moment she continued.

"Dr. Gorgas was in charge of Military Hospital Number One. He and Major John Davis, who was chief sanitary officer then—I think Davis was sent to Manila, and then Gorgas took over from him—got busy. Dr. Gorgas told us he started in the little waterfront office that had been assigned to him. He organized clean-up crews and gave each one a wagon. Then he sent them out to shovel and sweep and carry away the filth of the streets first. Dr. Gorgas said that in one street men worked around the clock 90 hours before they got down to the road's surface."

Clara shook her head in disbelief.

"I heard about Gorgas when I was in Santiago," she said. "He had to leave. Got malaria and couldn't shake it. But before he left, he burned the whole village of Siboney. Thought he'd burn up the yellow fever, I guess. But it didn't make any difference. Slippery yellow jack eluded his efforts and struck out worse than ever."

"I think Dr. Gorgas often feels terribly frustrated," Winifred Lewis said. "Nothing he tries works. I heard him say once, 'Trying to conquer yellow jack is very humbling.' But he keeps on trying. He's like a stubborn mule and won't be budged."

"Well, after cleaning the streets," she continued her account, "he went after the hospitals. The Spaniards had taken over the hospitals for barracks and had pushed all the sick out onto the streets. Gorgas found them there. Some had died. Their rotten corpses were burned. Gorgas took back into the hospitals he had cleaned up those who were still alive and started to nurse them. Many that came into the hospitals had sores all over them, even on their faces." Winifred paused, remembering, then went on. "Next Dr. Gorgas rounded up all the orphans and old people and set up homes for them and petitioned Surgeon General Sternberg for food. Sternberg can't do enough to relieve the suffering. He sent everything Gorgas asked for. And Major General Wood—he's Military Governor of Cuba, you know—he's just as compassionate. Even if he is a tough old soldier. If Gorgas hadn't had the support of Sternberg and Wood he couldn't have done what he did."

"Somebody told me Sternberg was in Memphis during the '78 epidemic," Clara said. "If he was, he's seen suffering firsthand and knows what it's like. Well, what happened next?"

"Did you notice the newly paved streets? Dr. Gorgas' construction crews did that too, so the streets would be easy to hose down and keep clean. And he cleaned out sewers and installed new sewers where there had been none."

"But the hardest task was to get inside the houses and into the inner patios and courtyards to clean them up. They tell us there are 26,000 homes in Havana."

"I can believe Gorgas would have trouble entering private homes," Clara interjected. "Isn't there anti-American feeling here among the Cubans? To begin with, it was so strong in Santiago that I remember General Wood saying—he was in charge when I was

104

there—that he scarcely could find one Cuban to cooperate."

The girls laughed. "That's where the Gorgeous Doctor—that's what we call him—really shines. In the first place, his name. The people like his name. Gorgas. Sounds like it belongs to Cuba. Then the doctor himself. He _is_ gorgeous. Soft voice. Pleasant manner. Old-time courtesy. He takes time to explain things to people and reason with them. Calls on them in their homes. He's really Prince Charming."

It's genuine too," Nellie Lewis affirmed. "He really cares about his patients. And handsome. Just wait until you see him." She fluttered her eye lashes. "Dark hair. Dark eyes." She sighed. "Sure too bad he's married. And married to someone he's still madly in love with. 'My Marie,' he says when he talks about her to us. But 'Darling' and 'Love' when he addresses her directly."

"It's interesting," she continued. "Mrs. Gorgas says they seem to have been destined to work with yellow fever. Dr. Josiah Nott, who delivered Dr. Gorgas when he was born, was a yellow fever nut. Mrs. Gorgas says she can remember meeting him in later life and listening to him expound the theory that an insect was responsible for spreading yellow fever. Mrs. Gorgas herself was down with yellow fever when Dr. Gorgas was called in to treat her. He fell in love with her, and then he came down with the fever. She used to say jokingly that yellow fever was an usher at their wedding."

Clara smiled. "But did Dr. Gorgas' charm work on everybody when he started to clean up Havana?"

"No, in some cases he had to fine people. But after they had cleaned up their premises and kept them clean for three or four weeks, he gave them back their money. 'Fines are to teach, not punish,' he said. 'You've learned your lesson. Now you can have your money back.'"

Clara chuckled appreciatively.

"But the sad part is," Miss Olbrian said, "that in spite of the 600 inspections for cleanliness which Dr. Gorgas has been making daily, once again yellow fever seems to have tricked him. It's been disappointing, because the first six months after Havana was cleaned up there were only five cases. Gorgas thought he had the fever licked. The number of typhoid, typhus, and malaria cases dropped too. He sent this report to the States, and the magazines gloated in reporting the victories the street broom, the scrubbing brush, the incinerator, and the disinfection spray pump had accomplished. Then yellow jack flared up again. Queerly enough yellow fever has snatched more victims this year than for many a year. Our hospitals are filling up. That's why he sent out the call you answered for more nurses."

"I'm glad he did," Clara said. "Sometimes I feel like Dr. Gorgas. I hate so much what yellow fever does to people that I'd give anything to lick it. Besides," she laughed, "who wouldn't prefer spending the winter in Cuba rather than New York if you can?"

And with that the girls climbed into bed, turned off their lights and were soon asleep.■

12

Closing In on Yellow Jack

The next morning at breakfast a messenger brought a note for Clara. "Dr. Gorgas would like to meet you on the veranda of Las Animas Hospital at ten o'clock," the note read.

The messenger reappeared at quarter to 10 to escort Clara through the hospital to the doctors' veranda. As she stepped out onto the veranda, Clara drew back timidly. For seated there was, not only Dr. Gorgas, whom she recognized at once, but several other men.

"Ah, Miss Maass?" Dr. Gorgas said, arising and coming over to greet her with hand extended. "Welcome to Las Animas Hospital! We are in conference now, but let me introduce you to these men. Then, if you come back in an hour's time, we can confer together."

He led Clara into the circle of men who were on their feet.

"Major Walter Reed. A native of Virginia, a graduate of Bellevue, a professor of bacteriology in the Army Medical School in

Washington. Major Reed is head of the U. S. Army Yellow Fever Commission."

Clara found herself looking into strikingly beautiful blue eyes so expressive she would always remember them. Steel-bright, pure, questioning, and shining, and with deep compassion pooled in their depths. In her confusion she forgot to extend her hand, but instead curtsied. Major Reed's firm mouth relaxed. He smiled unexpectedly. He must be about 50, Clara guessed, noticing the grey in his neatly trimmed mustache. His reddish hair was parted in the middle. Tall and slender, he towered over Clara.

Dr. Gorgas indicated the next gentleman. "Dr. Aristides Agramonte, former assistant bacteriologist of the Health Department of New York. Agramonte is in charge of autopsies and of the pathological work."

Clara stared. "He's shaved off his beard since I saw him in Santiago," she observed to herself. "And he's gained weight." Dr. Gorgas interrupted her thoughts.

"I called Dr. Agramonte over from Santiago to aid us in our research."

"Dr. Agramonte probably will not remember me, but I remember him," she said. "I met him in Santiago." I should say, I bumped into him, she thought, recalling the incident and reddening.

Dr. Agramonte's eyebrows above his brown eyes knitted in question, trying to remember Clara.

"Dr. James Carroll. Jim is from Johns Hopkins. He has brought two of the newest, most powerful German microscopes with him to aid us in our bacteriological research."

Blue eyes twinkled unexpectedly, and white teeth flashed Clara a warm, shy welcome. Carroll took her hand by the fingers gently. "I am honored, Miss Maass," he murmured. Clara picked up his English accent. She looked at his very tall, thin figure, his receding hairline, his light red mustache, his projecting ears holding up gold-rimmed spectacles. Not the most handsome, she thought fleetingly. And probably a scientist through and through.

"Dr. Juan Guiteras, who is on the staff here at Las Animas."

108

"I believe Dr. Guiteras and I met in Santiago," Clara said. Dr. Guiteras bowed.

"And then I want you to meet the man to whom we all owe much." Dr. Gorgas' voice was warm and affectionate. He stepped over to a short, heavyset man, dressed in an immaculate white suit, his big head crowned with snowy white hair. Lavish sideburns gave added dignity. The elderly gentleman was polishing his small oval glasses with his white handkerchief. He slipped them on his nose and gently eased the delicate gold bows under his flowing hair and over his ears. Guileless kind blue eyes looked out at Clara.

"This is Dr. Carlos Finlay of Cuba," Dr. Gorgas said, sliding an arm around the shoulder of the elderly man. "I'll tell you all about him later."

Dr. Finlay, surprisingly, stammered a bit as he greeted Clara. Her ears identified a soft Scottish burr.

"Major Reed has just arrived back from Washington, and we're bringing him up to date on what has happened," Dr. Gorgas explained. Then, turning to Dr. Guiteras, he said, "Juan, maybe you can take Miss Maass to your office. Fetch her a cup of good Cuban coffee and then explain to her what we are doing."

Dr. Guiteras smiled. "My pleasure," he said, "come with me, Miss Maass."

"Welcome to Las Animas," Dr. Guiteras said when they were seated in his office. "We are happy to have one with as fine a record as yours on our staff. I think you will be pleased to be part of Las Animas too. We are proud of our record of caring for patients with communicable diseases and especially yellow fever. The most desperate cases are referred to us. In spite of this we have the lowest percentage of fatalities of all the hospitals, less than 21 percent. Dependientes, Covadonga, and Benefica all have higher losses than this in spite of the fact that their cases are much less severe, and their patients, being members of clubs to which these hospitals belong, usually have been in good health previously. We get all races and all status of life here. But we attribute our success largely to the skilled nursing care we give our patients. We have not found drugs to be particularly helpful, so we rarely give medicine.

But we emphasize absolute rest, very careful dieting, and the constant attention, day and night, of trained nurses. So you see, Miss Maass, what an important and responsible position you will fill."

"I'm glad I could come," Clara said.

An aide arrived with coffee. Dr. Guiteras filled their cups.

"You know, of course," he continued, "that we are absorbed in a search to find out what is causing yellow fever. You were in Santiago . . ."

"And Manila," Clara added.

"And Manila too? Well, then you've seen the yellow killer at work." He settled back in his chair. "Actually the search has been going on for over 50 years. Way back in 1848 Dr. J. C. Nott of Mobile, in a paper entitled "On the Cause of Yellow Fever," suggested that insects play a part as carriers of yellow fever."

"Dr. Nott?" Clara interrupted. "Why last night one of the nurses was telling me that Dr. Nott was the physician who delivered Dr. Gorgas when he was born."

"Really?" Dr. Guiteras' eyebrows shot up. "Hmm. Interesting. Gorgas has never mentioned that to me. I know he was born in the South though. Mmm. Well," he went on, "a few years later Dr. Finlay—you met him this morning—who was president of the Superior Board of Health of Cuba at the time—began to formulate the first definite theory as to the transmission of yellow fever by means of a mosquito. He published his first paper Aug. 11, 1887. Finlay continued to pursue his theory for the next 10 years, modifying some of his ideas as the years went by. A couple of fellows, Dr. Domingo Freire of Rio de Janeiro and Dr. Carmona y Valle of Mexico, claimed to have isolated the bacterium causing yellow fever, but Dr. Sternberg, after careful investigation, proved their findings not true. Sternberg himself did some examination of blood of yellow fever cases in Havana but could determine nothing. All of this led to Sternberg appointing the Yellow Fever Commission, with Major Reed as chairman, to pinpoint definitely the cause of yellow fever. Major Reed feels now, however, that while we should not abandon our search for the cause of the disease, we should concentrate first on finding out how the disease spreads from ill patients to those who are well. This is what has caused us to consider again Nott and Finlay's theory about the mosquito. I fear, however, our search is going to be costly." He got up abruptly and began to pace the floor.

"I don't know if you've heard or not, but just a month ago, Tuesday, Sept. 25, to be exact, one of our team members died of it. Dr. Jesse Lazear. A prince of a fellow. Lazear was born of gentle folk in Baltimore. Kind, affectionate, dignified, with a high sense of honor, a staunch friend, and a faithful soldier. Had studied in Europe. Was a classmate of Agramonte's at Columbia University. Agramonte's taking it hard. Lazear came here with his microscope looking for guilty bacteria."

"He volunteered to be bitten?" Clara asked.

"Well, no. He told Agramonte his getting yellow fever was accidental, that he was bitten by a mosquito when he was performing an experiment, trying to get a mosquito to feed on an infected man. While he was holding a test tube with a mosquito in it on the man's stomach, another mosquito settled on his inner arm. Said he didn't shoo the mosquito away because he was afraid the movement would disturb the mosquito in the test tube who was busy getting his dinner. But Major Reed, who feels terrible about his death, was saying today that he wonders if Lazear let himself be bitten by an infected mosquito on purpose. He was wanting to check out some of the theories we've been playing around with. Like ascertaining when a patient is infectious. Major Reed thinks Lazear felt guilty about running tests on other humans without his being willing to submit first." He paused and wiped the perspiration from his forehead.

"You see, when we first realized we were going to have to experiment on humans, we all said we'd be willing to volunteer first. But, as it turned out, of our team, Agramonte's immune. Had it when he was a little kid here in Cuba. Reed was called back to Washington. That left Lazear and Carroll. So Lazear said, 'I'll try.' He let himself be bitten, but nothing happened. He didn't get sick that first time.

"Then some army fellows, who thought it was all a joke and who said they'd get it sooner or later so they might as well get it sooner, volunteered. This particular day Lazear had spent all morning getting infected mosquitoes to bite these volunteers. Real choosey old ladies, these mosquitoes are. Don't want to bite where there is any hair. Prefer to have it a little dark too. Well, Lazear had this one old lady mosquito who wasn't cooperating. Lazear was upset because she was particularly valuable having previously fed on four yellow fever patients. But this day when she refused to bite anyone, Lazear finally gave up and carried her back to the laboratory. As he was putting her tube on the rack he complained to Carroll who was working in the lab, 'She needs to eat to live,' he said, 'but she won't feed.' Lazear and Carroll went off to lunch, and when they came back Carroll said, 'Maybe she'd like a dinner from me. Isn't it my turn to volunteer?' And he bared his arm. He himself held the tube against his own arm and had to hold it quite a while before the old lady finally fed. Dr. Reed reminded Carroll today of the letter Carroll wrote him that night. 'If there's anything to the mosquito theory, I should get a good dose,' he wrote. 'That old lady should be lethal having dined on four of yellow jack's victims.'" Guiteras paused, staring off into space, then went on.

"Two days later, on Aug. 31, Carroll said he wasn't feeling well. The third day he was shaking with chills and burning with fever. By the time Agramonte and Gorgas got to him he was flip-flopping across the bed—he's a tall guy, you know. His fever shot up, his eyes burned livid, his tongue furred. Then he turned a saffron color as yellow as an oat field ripe for the sickle. Sometimes wild delirium controlled him. Sometimes he collapsed limp and seemingly lifeless. For three days we fought for his life. Lena Warner—have you met her yet in the nurses' quarters?—nursed him tirelessly. Carroll worried so about his family that we sent cables daily to his wife and five children a thousand miles away. But, sick as he was, he pleaded with us to let mosquitoes bite him, so we could use those mosquitoes for experiments."

Clara was leaning forward in her chair. Guiteras wiped his forehead again.

112

"Well, miraculously Carroll recovered. About two weeks after Carroll had gotten sick, Agramonte and Lazear were in the lab together, looking at the test tubes of mosquitoes that had fed on Carroll. They had been studying a report of Dr. Henry Carter. Carter had been conducting some experiments in Mississippi. He noticed that there often was a space of two or three weeks between cases. He concluded that something, an insect perhaps, carried the disease from person to person. But before the insect's bite became deadly the germ or bacteria or virus or whatever had to go through an incubation period inside of the insect. He guessed that incubation period to be two or three weeks."

Dr. Guiteras, who had been sitting down, got up, paced back and forth, lit a cigar, and then sat down again.

"Agramonte and Lazear were talking about this. 'Carroll got yellow fever when we let an infected mosquito bite him,' they said. 'So it looks as if the mosquito is the scoundrel who carries the killer. It's been two weeks since Carroll got sick. Carter thought the incubation period was two weeks or more. Wonder what would happen if we let one of those Carroll-infected mosquitoes bite someone else. Would that prove Carter's incubation theory? They were standing speculating when an army fellow, William H. Dean of Troop B, Seventh Cavalry, poked his head in the laboratory.

"'You still foolin' around with mosquitoes?' he asked.

"Agramonte and Lazear's eyes questioned each other. 'Would you like a bite?' Lazear asked, trying to sound casual, like he was asking, 'Would you like a cup of coffee?'

"'Why not?' Dean said. 'Those little mosquitoes don't scare me.'

"Lazear's eyes sought Agramonte's for an answer. Agramonte nodded ever so slightly.

"So they let the mosquito bite Dean, and five days later he was down with yellow fever. Lazear and Agramonte were jubilant. I remember walking in on Lazear in the lab. 'Aha, my pretty,' Lazear was upset, though, because Carroll had so nearly died, so he sisters like kittens, and after you've had a long enough resting time you turn out to be cobras on the wing. So that's it, eh?'

"Fortunately Dean too recovered. We wired the news to Reed in Washington. Major Reed was pretty happy to get the news. He was upset, though, because Carroll had so nearly died, so he forbade any more men on the team to volunteer. 'We can't afford to lose any scientists,' he said.

"He also thought we would have to produce more cases to definitely prove our point. Major Reed thinks that's why Lazear allowed himself to be bitten.

"One thing we haven't been sure of, you see, is when a patient is infectious. Why do some mosquitoes that bite yellow fever patients pass the fever along to others and some don't? Lazear was struggling with that puzzle. The mosquito that bit Lazear had bitten a man down with the fever three days, we've discovered."

He sat silent for a while, staring at a point beyond Clara's right shoulder. Finally he spoke again.

"Before Lazear entered the yellow fever ward he gave all his notes to Carroll and also passed on to him personal experience he had not yet recorded. Carroll was saying this morning he'll never forget the expression of alarm in Lazear's eyes the third and fourth day of his illness. His diaphragm was contracting spasmodically, and he knew this meant the black vomit was impending.

"Lena nursed him. Lena's lived through a lot. She went through the '78 epidemic in Grenada. Have her tell you about it. Lena said that when Lazear's black vomit began, it spurted out of his mouth up through the bar of his cot. Like a geyser. He was wild with delirium. The last night we took turns, two by two, holding him in bed. By morning he was dead." Guiteras blew his nose vigorously, walked over to the window and stood staring out. When he spoke again his voice was husky.

"He was only 34. Lived only seven days after he came down with the fever." He came over to his desk and pounded it with his fist. "Left a wife and two children. Kept talking right up to the last about not wanting to have this then-unborn second child come into the world fatherless. Real sad, it was." Guiteras stood, hitting the open palm of his left hand with his clenched right fist.

"So you've identified the mosquito as the carrier of yellow fever?" Clara asked excitedly.

"Well, yes and no. We're almost sure the mosquito carries yellow fever, but we still have to prove it conclusively." He began to pace again. "We've had to eliminate other theories first."

"Dr. Gorgas, for example, has been very skeptical of the mosquito theory. He thought cleaning up the city would take care of the problem. But we've had more cases this year than for many a year. So we've had to accept the fact that yellow fever isn't caused by poor sanitation, although I think Dr. Gorgas still clings to that theory and hasn't really accepted the mosquito theory yet.

"Dr. Reed earlier had asked us to check out the report of an Italian scientist who claimed that a bacterium called <u>Salmonella icteroides</u> caused yellow fever. Agramonte and Carroll spent hours hunched over their microscopes. Finally Carroll verified that <u>Salmonella icteroides</u> was the bacterium of hog cholera. So that removed another fallen log from the road.

"But now Dr. Reed wants us to test as to whether fomites are responsible or not. You know what fomites are?" darting a glance at Clara.

Clara nodded. "You mean the soiled clothing and blankets of infected men?"

"Right. That's what they were discussing when you walked in. They want to build a camp fairly close to Camp Columbia, both so we can bring in supplies and also so we can bring any yellow fever cases that might develop to the military hospital. Major Reed has suggested a farm named San Jose, belonging to Dr. Ignacio Rojas of Havana. It lies securely hidden off the road leading to Marianao. The ocean breezes blow fresh there. We want to name this experimental camp Camp Lazear." His voice trailed off again.

"This camp, what will you do at the camp?" Clara's question recalled Guiterans from his reverie about his dead colleague.

"Ah, yes, the camp. Plans are to pitch seven army tents in an arc. Those who supervise the experiments will stay in those. Then they'll build two small frame buildings about 80 yards apart. They'll make the buildings mosquito-proof, two thicknesses of walls and doors, lined with cotton batting to plug up all the cracks. They'll offer bonuses of from $100 to $200 for volunteers."

"For soldiers getting on the average of $15 a month that's going to be tempting," Clara said. "Especially when they know they might get the fever anyway."

"We'll have to get money for the experiment first," said Guiteras, sounding a little worried. "The men were discussing that. Surgeon General Sternberg still thinks the mosquito theory absurd. It's questionable he would give us a grant now, especially after Lazear's death. He frowns on experimenting on humans."

"How much do you need?"

"$10,000 at least."

Clara gave a little gasp.

Guiteras went on. "Dr. Kean, who has been working with our board, thinks we should approach Wood."

"When I was in Santiago," Clara said, "I heard over and over how committed General Wood is to wiping out yellow fever."

"Yes, here too he says repeatedly that if we can get at the cause of yellow fever, or at least discover how it is spread, that achievement would be of more importance to Cuba and the rest of the world than anything else we could do."

"To get back to your experiment," Clara said, "what do you propose to do?"

"They'll put three nonimmune men in a 14 x 20 foot room in one of the buildings, to sleep in the most horribly soiled bedding we can get. Sheets that have been vomited all over."

Clara's nose twitched.

"To make doubly sure they are infected, Reed proposes pouring basins of vomit and excreta on the bedding and the night clothing the men will wear. The room will be darkened so light will not disinfect the fomites. A coal oil stove with a pan of water will keep the temperature 95 degrees and the humidity high. The volunteers will stay there for 20 days."

Clara ran a hand across her forehead.

"The other building will have two rooms. Everything in that building will be clean. The ocean breezes will blow through. But we'll turn loose yellow fever-infected mosquitoes in one room. One volunteer will enter that room. And we'll see what happens."

"Oh, my goodness!" Clara exclaimed.

"I know. None of us like experimenting with people. But we're engaged in a war, and in a war we have to be prepared for loss of life."

"I understand," said Clara. She was silent for a while. Then standing up she said, "Dr. Guiteras, if I can be of any service, I am ready." Her voice was a bit unsteady but determined.

Dr. Guiteras who had been sitting with his arms crossed and his hands tucked into his armpits, jerked erect. He stared at her.

"No!" he cried out. "No, no! You must understand the risks! Better that you care for the sick. No, no!" His voice was agitated.

Clara opened her mouth as though to say something more. Then she wheeled about abruptly and ran from the room.■

BOTTOM LEFT: Telegram sent to Maass family by Dr. Gorgas, Oct. 14, 1900. Clara Maass was seriously ill; BOTTOM RIGHT: Dr. Gorgas, Chief Sanitary Officer, Cuba; MIDDLE LEFT: Dr. Lazear, Yellow Fever Researchist; MIDDLE RIGHT: Lazear Hut where the experiments in connection with the fomites was conducted; TOP RIGHT: Las Animas Hospital in the late 1800's, Havana, Cuba; TOP LEFT: Newspaper announcement regarding Clara Maass' death in the NEW YORK HERALD.

13

Yellow Jack's Accomplice Tracked Down

A few days later a jubilant Dr. Guiteras broke the news to Clara that Wood had given them the grant needed for their experiments.

"Dr. Kean told me about it," he related joyously. "He himself took Major Reed to Governor Wood's office in the old palace. Dr. Kean said Reed and Wood stood framed in a window that looked out on the Plaza de las Armas. Between the two men, Kean said, he could see grey, weather-beaten Morro Castle, the blue waters of the harbor, and the ancient fort, Las Fuerza, built by De Soto before he sailed northward to find the Mississippi. There these two Americans stood: Wood, powerful, leonine, impassive; Reed, slender, alert, enthusiastic. Both medical doctors. Both military officers. Reed spoke earnestly, telling Wood about Lazear and Carroll, the need for more conclusive research, and their need of funds.

"'How much?' Kean heard Wood ask.

"'Ten thousand,' replied Reed.

"'It's yours,' said Wood. 'I have this morning signed a warrant for that amount to aid the police in the capture of criminals. This work is of more importance to Cuba than the capture of a few thieves. I will give you $10,000. If that proves insufficient, I will give you $10,000 more.

"Wood's one concern," Guiteras said, looking sharply at Clara, "is that only sound persons of full legal age who understand the risk and accept it in writing, be allowed to participate in the experiments. If Spaniards volunteer, they are to get the consent of the Spanish consul. If we observe these stipulations, Wood promises us the full support of the government."

And so work on the experiments went forward. The buildings were built and the tents pitched. Agramonte was to supervise the signing up of Spanish immigrant volunteers and Reed the Americans. Guiteras kept Clara informed as to what was going on.

The very first morning, he related, two young men, John R. Kissinger and John J. Moran, had presented themselves to Major Reed.

"You understand the risks?" Reed had asked, scrutinizing them as he described in detail every phase of suffering they could experience if the disease gripped them.

The men had not flinched.

Reed had gone on to explain the monetary arrangements.

"Sir," Kissinger had replied, drawing himself erect, "we don't want the money. We offer ourselves solely in the interest of humanity and the cause of science."

Reed, Guiteras confided, was overcome. Though he was a Major and Kissinger only a private and Moran a civilian clerk, Reed arose, touched his hat and saluted them.

Friday evening, Nov. 30, the fomite-infected building was ready for use. The next day Dr. Agramonte, visiting Las Animas Hospital, described what had happened to a small group of doctors and nurses. Clara listened intently to his account.

"Dr. Robert Cook, Acting Assistant Surgeon of the U. S. Army, believes the mosquito theory so completely he volunteered to be one of the first in the infected building. Two other Americans, Folk and Jernigan, went with him. They had instructions to unpack the boxes and trunk, to handle and shake the clothing and in every way to disseminate the yellow fever poison in case it was contained in the various pieces. We peered through one of the windows and watched. Suddenly the door was flung open, and the three men fell all over each other as they rushed from the room out into the fresh air. One of the men doubled over and vomited all over the place. But after a few minutes, gathering courage and determination, they went back into the building. This morning we called to them through the window. They hadn't slept, they said, and the stench was unbelievable."

For 20 nights the men slept in the fomite-infected building. During the day, under strict quarantine, they were allowed to be in a screened-in tent. At the end of the time the men were healthy and well, in fact, they had even gained weight.

However, an ominous though conclusive report had come from the other building.

This building had two rooms, carefully screened, one from the other. The only furniture was four cots—a single cot in the larger room and three cots in the smaller room. Dec. 21 three young nonimmune men, who had been in quarantine 32 days, entered the smaller sterile room. That same day at noon 15 mosquitoes were freed in the larger room. Five minutes later Moran, clad only in his night shirt and fresh from a bath, entered the mosquito-laden room and threw himself down on the cot. For 30 minutes he lay there. Infectious mosquitoes promptly settled on him and bit him on his face and hands. Seven bit him on his first visit. At 4:30 p.m. he entered the room again and stayed 15 minutes. He was bitten five times. The next day at 4:30 p.m. he again reentered the room and was bitten three times, a total of 15 bites. The building was then closed.

In the smaller room of the building were two nonimmunes who did not enter the mosquito room. The two nonimmunes remained healthy. Christmas morning at 11 a.m. yellow fever attacked young Moran, and he was removed to the hospital.

New Year's Eve Dr. Walter Reed sat in his room at Columbia Barracks and wrote his wife, Emilie, a letter:

"My assistants and I have at last been permitted to lift the impenetrable veil that so long has surrounded the causation of this dreadful pest of humanity, and to put it on a rational, scientific basis. I thank God that this has been accomplished. . . . The prayer that has been mine for the last twenty years—that I might be permitted in some way to alleviate the suffering of mankind—has been granted."

To substantiate their findings, the commission next arranged for several more volunteers to be bitten by fever-infected mosquitoes. The results identified the mosquito as the carrier, and the men on the commission were gratified that all the volunteers recovered.

Over in the nurses' quarters some time later Clara and her colleagues were discussing the experiment.

"The world will long remember Major Walter Reed," one said.

"Ever notice," Clara observed, "how humble the man is? 'Don't bother with the Major bit,' he says, 'just call me doctor.'"

"I think of a line from Kipling when I think of Dr. Reed," Lena Warner, the oldest nurse in the group said. "' . . . so walked he from his birth—in simpleness and gentleness and honour and clean mirth.'"

"I know," Clara agreed quickly. "Do you remember the day he moved his mess quarters because the officers were using language at the table he considered inappropriate?"

"I always marvel at how interested he is in common people," Lena went on. "Many a time he's called me over to the mircroscope and let me look and explained things I hadn't understood."

"I know," Clara said, "he makes a nurse feel as though she's a real team member of the experiment."

"One day," Lena reflected, "we were looking in the microscope together. 'Lena,' he said suddenly, 'many years ago when I was just a young doctor I was appointed district physician to

122

one of the poorer districts in New York. Day after day I saw poverty and misery firsthand. I remember coming home late one night after I had made several house calls in the tenement section. I stood at the window looking out at the clean, well-lighted streets, and the fine houses in the area where we lived. Suddenly I found myself on my knees praying. Since that day, Lena, I have cherished one great dream only—to be able to do some small thing to relieve the suffering of humanity. Do you suppose, Lena, in these yellow fever experiments my prayer might be granted?"

"He is a religious man," one of the younger nurses said. "Some of the soldiers think he's too strict. He won't let any of his officers touch liquor."

"But I know of men who have thanked him for that rule," Lena said quickly. "And I have the feeling later in life they'll be even more grateful. And think of the misery and suffering people will be spared if yellow fever can be wiped out."

"You were in Grenada during the '78 epidemic, weren't you?" Clara asked, remembering Dr. Guiteras' words to her earlier.

Lena nodded. "That was my first great sorrow. In my own family eight members were stricken. I and another nine-year-old child were the only ones who recovered. You've read about The Howards, haven't you, the people who volunteered to come and nurse and help?"

The girls nodded.

"Well, unfortunately, there were unscrupulous, greedy people around too. Some disguised themselves as Howards in order to gain entrance into homes. My own father, who was down with the fever, was choked, robbed, and left alone to die. I saw it all but was too sick even to cry out for help. I lay there for 20 hours with my dead father before someone found us."

Her voice died away and the room was plunged into quietude. Finally Clara broke the silence.

"How do you think Dr. Gorgas feels about having his sanitation theory disproved?" she asked, changing the subject. "I was told that during the clean-up campaign the Havanese laughed at him. The cleaner the city got, the more yellow fever cases appeared at the hospital. Now others could laugh if they wanted to. Think of all those magazine articles."

"I don't think Gorgas is convinced even yet," Miss Olbrian said. "But in regard to the increase of cases lately, haven't you heard Dr. Finlay's explanation? He reminded us of all the immigrants who have poured into the city the last months, from Spain, the Canary Islands, Mexico, and South America. Five hundred in July. Nearly 1,000 in August. The immigrants were nonimmunes. Doc Finlay warned us we could expect an epidemic." epidemic."

"I really haven't learned to know Dr. Finlay," Clara said. "I see him often in the hospital, but that's all. He seems to be a kindly, cheerful, and very patient old gentleman."

"Oh, he's a dear!" Winifred Lewis enthused. "For over 20 years he has been trying to tell people that the Culex fasciatus— that was its name then—mosquito carried the yellow fever bacteria or virus or whatever it is that causes the fever. But no one would take him seriously. Even Dr. Gorgas, who is such a close friend of his, called his theory 'absurd.' Dr. Finlay even went to General Wood. The story goes around that when he talked with Wood he quoted Oliver Wendell Holmes and said, 'I am too much in earnest for either humility or vanity, but I do entreat those who hold the keys of life and death to listen to me for this once.' Wood did listen and later pored over all Finlay's articles which had been published in reputable medical journals. He wasn't convinced then, but I'm sure it all made an impression on Wood.

"It's really remarkable how Dr. Finlay refused to be discouraged. He just kept on raising mosquitoes and carrying one around in his test tube and talking to everybody new who turned up in town. I remember last year when Gorgas thought he had licked yellow fever with his sanitation efforts, old Doc Finlay walked around and shook his test tube under the noses of everyone around him and kept exclaiming, 'Just one case is like a lighted match that is dropped on dry shavings.'"

"They nicknamed him 'Cuba's mosquito man,' didn't they?" The nurse who spoke had just brought in a jug of lemonade for the

124

girls. She set it down on the table. "Remember the time he spoke to us nurses? He brought the mosquito Madame Stegomyia, as he called her, with him and told us all about her. I still remember some of her characteristics."

"I do too. She's a city gal. Delicate. Hates the light. Hides behind pictures and draperies, under beds and in closets and clothing."

"Is sly," Lena added. "Sneaks up on you. Doesn't sing a warning but feeds silently. Likes it warm and quiet. Has a marked preference for human blood. Likes to breakfast at dawn, sleep through the day, and have dinner at twilight. Doesn't eat at night unless someone turns on the light."

"Remember what she looked like? A black and white beauty with a lyre tattooed on her back."

"But hadn't Dr. Finlay conducted any experiments to prove his theory?" Clara asked.

"Oh, yes, he had fed his mosquitoes on over 100. But only a few had contracted the fever and no clear-cut pattern seemed to emerge from his results. He couldn't persuade doctors. What Dr. Finlay didn't understand, and what we are beginning to understand only now, is that a mosquito must bite a victim during the first three, four, or possibly even five days of the fever's course in order to pick up the infectious germ. This is one of the conclusions that came out of these recent experiments. And then another 12 days or more must elapse during which time the germ incubates inside the mosquito. Only as she bites a human after that time will the person be infected and become ill."

"Dr. Lazear started to explain this to me the first day I came," Clara said. "It's fascinating, like putting together a puzzle."

"I'm so glad that at last Doc Finlay is going to get some credit for his work," Lena said. "Have you heard? Seventy or 80 physicians of Havana are going to have a banquet in his honor."

"That's great," Clara agreed. "But the battle's not completely won yet, is it? They're almost convinced now—except Dr. Gorgas—that the mosquito is the carrier, but what does she carry? Bacterium? Or virus? Dr. Carroll has been hunched over his microscope again trying to isolate the culprit, but he has just about decided it is nonfilterable."

"And until we can discover the prime cause, how can we stop yellow fever?" Miss Olbrian asked worriedly. She swished out her hand, closed her fist tight, and then opened it. Three dead mosquitoes lay in her palm. "There are hundreds of these flying around. Which one is guilty? And who is going to get rid of all these mosquitoes? Impossible!"

And the elation with which the girls had been discussing the success of the experiments evaporated.■

14

Parabolani

The work of the Yellow Fever Commission was considered finished. Reed and Carroll returned to Washington. Before they left they presented Dr. Gorgas with the lone <u>Stegomyia</u> that remained from the supply of mosquitoes they had used for experiments.

"Her Ladyship is old and a bit tired," Reed said. "But she has served well. If you can find further use for her, she is yours. Winter is coming. You won't be able to find any more around until next summer."

Gorgas frowned. He had always cherished misgivings about the experiments at Las Animas Hospital and Camp Lazear. Life was too precious to conduct experiments that might extinguish someone's life.

"Thank you for the mosquito," he said a bit stiffly. "I shall take good care of her. But if it is true, as you say, that the mosquito carries yellow fever, personally I think I prefer killing mosquitoes rather than men."

Winter's chill was seeping into Las Animas Hospital. Conscientious about his promise to care for the old lady mosquito, Dr. Gorgas ordered an oil stove from the U. S. to heat the room where she was. Confined to a large glass jar Her Ladyship was fed sugar, bananas, and water. But in spite of the fastidious care given her, Her Ladyship brought about her own end. Flitting about her jar one day one of her wings caught in the fine mesh at the top of the jar. All the Las Animas medical staff crowded around and with fine forceps tried to free the fragile wing. But the shock was too much for the old lady, and at 9 a.m. she died.

"What will this mean?" asked Clara, who found herself standing next to Dr. Gorgas. For the first time she noticed a few silver streaks in his black hair.

He hesitated momentarily.

"Dr. Guiteras and I have been discussing the possibility of developing a vaccine to immunize people against yellow fever," he said slowly. "Edward Jenner in England developed a cowpox vaccine against smallpox, you will remember. We've been wondering if we could do the same for yellow fever."

"You mean you would have to induce yellow fever first?" Clara asked.

Dr. Gorgas' dark eyes brooded. "There seems no alternative," he said. "Animals seem immune." He paused, then said, almost roughly, "I don't like the idea of experimenting with humans. It's risky. Though, of course, all of the last cases Reed's Commission induced were light—but I still don't like it! Never mind. With Her Ladyship gone, we'll have to wait for the warm summer months to capture some more Stegomyia. The delay will give us time to think and pray. And in he meantime I'm going to begin to try and rid Havana of mosquitoes."

The cool winter months brought fewer patients to the hospital, and the nurses were able to get time off regularly. One Sunday when Clara went to the small Episcopal church, she was surprised to see Dr. Gorgas sitting up front in the vicar's chair.

At the time of announcements he counseled the worshipers to be present the next Sunday, when at the early morning service the vicar would lead them in celebration of the Eucharist.

"I myself," he said, "find the Sacrament of the Lord's Supper most comforting." He paused, then repeated thoughtfully, "Most comforting."

His sermon was brief and simple. He read from the apostle Paul's letter to the Philippians. Paul was an old man, he explained, confined in Rome, probably on house imprisonment. His friends at Philippi had heard of his trouble. They had sent Epaphroditus, one of their community, both to carry their love gift of money to Paul and to spend some time with him, caring for him and cheering him up. But shortly after Epaphroditus arrived he became ill—so ill, Gorgas explained, that he was "nigh unto death." But, Gorgas pointed out, Paul had added, "God had mercy on him, and not on him only, but on me also that I might not have sorrow upon sorrow." Gorgas emphasized that as Paul closed his letter he admonished the Philippians to honor Epaphroditus, who was now returning to them, for, Paul declared, "he risked his very life for me."

The early Christians, Gorgas went on to say, had a name for all those who risked their lives. Parabolani this community of men and women were called—"The Gamblers." To haunts of wretchedness and disease the parabolani went, visiting the prisoners, loving the outcastes, caring especially for the sick with contagious diseases, risking infection by living even among the lepers. In A.D. 252 plague broke out in Carthage. The people flung out from their houses those who had died and then fled in terror. Cyprian, the Christian bishop at that time, called together the parabolani. Risking their own lives, they buried the dead, nursed the sick, and comforted the bereaved. Without their selfless care the whole city possibly would have been wiped out.

The world still needed parabolani, Gorgas told his small congregation. "As for me," he assured them, "I hope I can go on pouring out my life for others until the very end. I hope," and his dark eyes twinkled, "like the old soldier, I can die with my boots on."

Death, he said, held few fears for him, for he expected, because of the love and sacrifice of his Lord, to live beyond the grave.

"I hope to meet all of you there," he said. "I like to believe that in the life to come both you and I will again take up our work to do our mite toward helping to finish out the great scheme the Almighty has established. I like to think that we will have the same free will for making or marring that we have had in this world, and that there we may be employed to correct some of the faults that we have made down here."

All the way back to Las Animas Hospital Clara turned over in her mind the words of her doctor and found her heart profoundly stirred.

During the month of May Dr. Guiteras began his search for Stegoymia mosquitoes with which he would be able to conduct his experiments.

Dr. Gorgas was busily at work on his own project of eliminating mosquitoes from Havana. He enforced the isolation of all yellow fever patients, screened the houses, and then set about to exterminate the mosquitoes. If in his heart he was lukewarm in his endeavor because he did not yet fully believe the mosquito was at fault, his outward actions did not betray him.

Using the same techniques he had used earlier to rid Havana of filth, he now sought to rid the city of any stagnant water where mosquitoes could breed. He organized his inspection teams and sent them out. In Havana, where almost daily showers left puddles, he ordered the men to pour a film of kerosene on the puddles. He obtained a ruling from the Havana City Council that all gutters had to be cleaned out, all empty tin cans, flower pots, or anything in which water might collect must be tipped upside down. Water stored in containers must be covered. Attention did not need to be paid to large pools or bodies of water nor to flowing water, for the Stegomyia, or Aëdes aegypti, as she was also called, did not breed there.

Patiently Gorgas met all the angry Cubans who stormed into his office. Calmly he explained why a cat's water dish could not stand around, why, at least for a while, the goldfish pools on the patios would have to be drained. In the tropics the legs of tables and food storage cupboards and bedposts sit in little tins of water to prevent ants from climbing up. These tins, Gorgas insisted, must either be emptied or have kerosene poured into them. He begged, coaxed, cajoled, explained, and, when he had to, fined. The Cubans rebelled, grew angry, refused to cooperate, laughed, and finally listened to him.

June arrived, sweltering and hot. The heat was not confined to the weather. Warm discussions flared between Dr. Guiteras and Dr. Gorgas. Clara sometimes would catch snatches as she passed Dr. Gorgas' office.

"I'm not at all sure we should try it, Juan."

"But if we don't develop a vaccine, how will we ever lick yellow fever?"

"I know. But I still don't like using humans in experiments."

Guiteras won out. He announced the beginning of the program and called for volunteers—$100 for volunteering, $200 if you contract the disease.

One of the first ones in his office was Clara. When she stated why she had come, Guiteras frowned. His dark skin grew darker.

"I've thought about it for months," Clara said hurriedly, trying to forestall his objections. "I'd be really happy if I could do something to prevent others from getting yellow fever. Besides," she added honestly, "Mother can use the money." She blushed. "I'm planning to return to the U.S. to get married. I've thought of bringing my sister, Sophie down here to take over my job. With the $50 she'll earn a month, and the money I can send Mother from these experiments, she should be able to pay off her debts and take care of the babies." She stopped. She wasn't used to talking about family matters, but she sensed persuading Dr. Guiteras was going to call for some arguing.

His frown grew deeper. "You're going to get married? . . . Forget it then!"

"No, no! With all the nursing of yellow fever patients I've done, I've never gotten it. I must be immune, don't you think? Or if I do get it, I'm sure it will be only a light case. Please. I really want to do it."

Dr. Guiteras arose, walked to his window and stood with his back to Clara.

She addressed his back. "I think it's a shame so few Americans have volunteered."

"I don't know why you don't accept a volunteer when one comes of her own volition."

Still no answer.

"I know how hard it was for you to get volunteers for the mosquito-laden buildings. I know how Dr. Agramonte went to Tiscornia, the Immigration Station across the Bay of Havana, every time a load of Spanish immigrants arrived. I know how he'd offer eight or ten of the men jobs as day laborers at the camp. But the job offer was really just a come-on, wasn't it?" Clara's voice grew heated.

"You can hardly call picking up a few loose stones a job, can you? But you let the men pick stones. You fed them well, saw to it that they had plenty of rest, had them sleep under mosquito nets, and then when you saw their health was good and their resistance built up, you began to talk to them. You told them how they could make lots of money, a hundred dollars, five hundred pesetas, by letting themselves be bitten by mosquitoes. You suggested that chances are sooner or later they would be bitten by mosquitoes anyway so why not get paid for it and receive the best care they could. Of course you didn't mention anything about who would pay for funeral expenses."

Dr. Guiteras' shoulders twitched.

"But then the Spaniards really didn't expect to get sick, much less die. If they had, why, when the first four cases came down with yellow fever and the other volunteers saw them being carried out of the camp to the hospital did the volunteers panic? Why did they bring back their 500 pesetas and throw them at your feet and say they wanted no part in these experiments."

Clara paused, drew a deep breath, then went on.

"You considered those Spaniards expendable. Aren't they of as much value as we Americans?"

132

Guiteras swung around. His swarthy skin had turned even darker.

"What we did was above board! We explained the risks, We had each one sign a statement. We called on the Spanish consul and explained what we were doing." He struck the counter with his fist so the test tubes in their racks rattled. "And not one of the volunteers died.

"And you forget! You forget Carroll. And Lazear. Have you forgotten Lazear paid the supreme price? And what about Kissinger? And Moran?"

"I know, I know," Clara soothed. "I'm only trying to tell you that if there are others of us Americans who want to volunteer, you should let us."

Guiteras flung his towel in the sink, and stood staring at it. "All right," he said finally. "All right. If that's the way you'll have it."

"Today?"

"No, tomorrow. Meet me here in the laboratory."

Clara turned to go.

"Miss Maass." The tone had changed. The anger was gone. "Yes?"

"Miss Maass—well, I feel like Major Reed. I'd like to salute you."

Clara smiled. "That," she said, "would be a unique honor for a nurse."

The next day, June 4, 1901, Clara arrived early to hear an agitated voice spilling out from the laboratory. She recognized it, in spite of its unusual highly perturbed tone, as belonging to Dr. Gorgas.

"I don't know if I approve!"

A low mumbled answer Clara couldn't catch.

"But Miss Maass of all people! She's one of the most loved nurses on the staff here. An excellent nurse. And a woman!"

Clara backed away and dodged into a supply room. She pulled the door shut and waited until she heard quick steps echo past her. When the corridor was silent, she opened the door and walked down to the laboratory.

Dr. Guiteras greeted her with a troubled look and a synthetic smile.

"Good morning!" Clara was determined to be cheerful.

"Miss Maass, you're sure you want to go through with this? You know the risks involved. Jim Carroll lived. Lazear—" Guiteras' voice sagged.

"I told you I've thought about this for months." Slight annoyance. "Where do you want me bitten?"

Guiteras reddened. "Well, I, uh, we've never done it on females before. I guess your forearm will do."

Resolutely Clara unbuttoned the long cuff of her sleeve and folded it back.

"Here," she said, thrusting out her arm.

Guiteras was coming back with a test tube from the rack on the cupboard. He lifted out the fluffy cotton batting plug and quickly tipped the tube over and pressed it against Clara's arm. The mosquito flew to the top. Guiteras tapped the top. The mosquito didn't move. He tapped it again. Uncertainly the mosquito moved downward, her transparent wings barely fluttering. She hovered over Clara's arm, then lightly landed. Gently she punctured the white flesh of Clara's slim arm with her steel-like thread-thin proboscis, located a capillary, and feasted.

"There!" said Guiteras when the mosquito, gorged at last, withdrew her beak and sluggishly flapped to the top of the tube. "Now we'll see what kind of a fighter you are!" His laugh was hollow.

"One bite isn't enough!" Clara protested.

Guiteras put the tube back on the rack. "I'm not giving you any more," he said stubbornly.

"Then I'll have to hold a tube myself," Clara said, reaching for one. "Maybe, while I'm at it, maybe I should give two or three ladies a dinner." She forced gaiety into her voice.

Guiteras turned his back. An uneasy silence hung between them.

"There!" Clara said at last. "Five bites. That should do it. Wonder if the little ladies will deliver the goods in time for my 25th birthday four days from now." Clara's tone was too jovial.

"Would you like that really?" Guiteras asked, keeping up the game of pretending.

But as Guiteras watched Clara's slender figure with the tiny waist disappear out the door, his darkskinned face clouded over again, and the worried frown reappeared.

That night, in her room, Clara sat down and wrote her mother a letter.

> I will soon send you $100. It will pay immediate debts and enable Sophie to come to Cuba. I can get her a position as a nurse here at $50 a month. She can take my place Mother, for—now don't be surprised—I am soon to be married.

Three days later at breakfast Nellie Lewis noticed that Clara sat listlessly, absentmindedly stirring the sugar in her coffee.

"Aren't you feeling well?" Nellie whispered apprehensively.

"Not the best. Bit of a headache. And feel a little chilly. But I'll be all right."

By 11 o'clock Clara asked permission to go home. Back in her room she sat down to write her mother another letter.

> Do not worry, Mother, if you hear that I have yellow fever. Now is a good time of the year to catch it if one has to. Most of the cases are mild, and then I should be immune and not afraid of the disease anymore.

She addressed the envelope, sealed, and stamped it. Then she went out to mail it. When she came back, she crawled into bed. ∎

15

Yellow Jack Claims Another Victim

Clara's case fortunately was light. Within a week's time she was back in the wards, in high spirits, exulting because from now on and forever she would be immune. She began to count the days until fall, when she planned to leave.

Torrid July was surpassed only by sticky, humid August. Guiteras seemed to lag in his experiments.

"Can't you use my blood?" Clara kept asking.

Finally Guiteras answered her straightforwardly. "Frankly, I think your case was too light for you to be immune. I don't think your blood is of sufficient value, and I don't know how much immunity you yourself have."

"Really?" Astonishment.

A couple of days later Clara reappeared in the laboratory.

"I want to try again," she announced.

"Again?" Guiteras eyebrows shot up.

"Why not? I surely have enough immunity to guarantee a light case. And two light attacks should be good for something."

Guiteras shook his head.

"I'm serious."

Guiteras stiffened. "I can't let you."

"It's my choice." Then changing her tone, "I'm sure it'll be all right."

Guiteras resisted.

Clara leaned across the table. Her voice was intense. "Can't you understand? I really want to do this. I saw so many men die in Manila," her voice broke. "If I can do anything—anything at all—"

Guiteras turned away abruptly. Going over to his sink he began to wash test tubes. He washed vigorously. Soapsuds flew as he viciously drew the brush in and out. The test tubes sparkled. Next he tackled the counters. He scrubbed till they shone. After the counters he began to scour the sink.

"Please." Clara's coaxing voice intruded.

Guiteras scrubbed on. Finally he rinsed his hands, wiped them, hung up the towel, and then turned. He didn't look at Clara and his voice was rough.

"You are stubborn." He stood playing with his mustache. Then, "I already have seven coming in at 8 a.m. tomorrow. You really don't have to volunteer."

"I'll be here." Clara's voice was triumphant, yet something in it caused Guiteras to look at her. Her eyes were full of tears.

And so it was that on Wednesday, Aug. 14, 1901, at 9 a.m., Clara laid bare her arm again and was bitten twice.

Four mornings later Clara awakened at 6 a.m. to find herself shaking. She pulled up the blankets around her shoulders. And then, as consciousness dawned as to what was happening, she sat up and reached over into her drawer for her thermometer.

She was shaking pretty badly. She worried lest her chattering teeth bite through the glass.

She felt around in her drawer for her round, gold watch. She flipped open the cover, then watching the second hand, with the fingers of her right hand she probed for the radial artery on her left wrist.

"Pulse 80," she noted. "Better start my own chart."

She dug out a piece of paper from the drawer, wrote "Aug. 18," and entered her temperature and pulse. Then she crept under the blankets. The fever should arrive any minute now, she said to herself.

The chill left. She felt quite comfortable. Maybe I imagined it, she thought. Maybe I should get up and get dressed after all.

Then she felt the rosy warmth begin to steal over her. Soon the heavy army blankets were too hot. She threw them back. She reached for the thermometer, checked her pulse and recorded: "Temperature 100F., pulse 90 beats a minute."

Her roommate awakened in time to see her putting away the thermometer.

"You sick?" Alarm in her voice.

"Not really. But I think I'll rest."

"Can I bring you anything for breakfast."

"Just toast and coffee please."

Dr. Gorgas appeared unexpectedly with the breakfast tray.

"Feel any dizziness?" He gave her a definitive glance.

"No."

"Any nausea or pain over the stomach?" His voice was sharp with concern.

"No."

"Limbs ache?"

"No, I'm just tired."

He checked her temperature and pulse. "Drink lots of water," he ordered. "I'll take a slide for malaria and be back at noon."

At noon Clara was twising on her bed. Her head throbbed until the ceiling she was staring at began to revolve.

"My calves and thighs ache," she complained. "And I feel as if someone was pressing a knife in my lower back."

"Miss Maass," Dr. Gorgas said firmly, but with infinite kindness, "we're moving you to the yellow fever ward."

In her hospital room Clara asked for a mirror. "My eyes are swollen," she said, "it isn't just that they feel that way."

By two in the afternoon Clara's fever had climbed to 102. Her pulse was 115.

"It really got you this time," Dr. Gorgas said. "You're going to have to fight back with all you've got."

"I feel like I have iron clamps over my temples," Clara complained, holding her head with her hands. "And the muscles in my calves are all knotted."

"I know," soothed the troubled surgeon by her bed. "I've had it too—remember?"

In the evening Clara turned her face away from the supper they brought her. When she tried to drink the water the nurse handed her, she found herself vomiting. But she felt better after she vomited, and her temperature started to drop.

She asked the nurse for some stationery and a pen. Propped up in bed, she wrote:

Good-bye, Mother. Don't worry. God will care for me in the yellow fever hospital the same as if I were at home. I will send you nearly all I earn, so be good to yourself and the two little ones [her youngest sisters]. You know I am the man of the family now, but do pray for me.

At around 10 Gorgas dropped in to see her again. His eyes scanned her chart, his hand felt her cool cheek.

"You're in phase two," he said. "You'll feel better the next 24 hours. Rest all you can."

But on the way home Dr. Gorgas stopped at the local telegraph office and awakened the proprietor.

"I want to sent a telegram to Miss Sophia Maass, East Orange, New Jersey," he said. "The message should read, 'Miss Maass has yellow fever,' and bear my signature."

During the night Clara's temperature dropped even more, but she was plagued by nightmares and kept awakening, shaking with fear.

By morning her temperature was normal, her pulse down to 80. Her body was sore and felt as it she had been beat up, but it no longer ached. Her eyelids had stopped burning.

By noon her temperature had climbed to 100 degrees. She

139

cried for water. She tossed restlessly. The aches and pains were returning. But surprisingly that night she slept well.

By noon the next day her temperature was 102 degrees. She couldn't bear the weight of the blankets. Her ribs pinched her. She felt heavy pressure on her back. By evening her temperature was 104 degrees.

"How bad is my jaundice?" she asked, her brain still clear enough to follow the progress of her disease. "My gums feel swollen."

"The strange thing about yellow fever," Dr. Gorgas said in a low-tone to Dr. Guiteras as they walked down the hallway away from Clara's room, "is that it tortures all the body save the brain. The liver, gone crazy, bombards blood and tissue with bile pigment. But the mind functions clearly, and the patient is fully aware of all that is going on."

She slept little that night. Nightmares plagued her again.

The next day, Saturday, Clara's temperature hovered around 103 degrees. The following day she complained to Gorgas of her stomach feeling small and hard like a billiard ball.

Gorgas left the room abruptly and walked quickly to his office. He reached for his phone and dispatched a second telegraphic message: "Miss Maass worse."

When he got back to her room she was vomiting. "Fly wings," her chart said. "Fly wings." The ominous dark specks that prefaced the arrival of the vomito negro!

Her nose started to bleed profusely. Her eyeballs and skin had turned a deep yellow. Hiccups convulsed her slight frame.

Gorgas stood by her bed, dabbing away vainly at the blood pouring from her nostrils. A shadow fell across the bed. Gorgas look up. So Guiteras had come.

A strange, gurgling noise arose from the bed. The slight figure lying there doubled up, next stiffened, and then arched up suddenly. A geyser of vile-smelling black liquid shot out, spraying both doctors who instinctively clapped hands over their mouths and noses and hastily backed off. Clara's eyes bulged. Then the geyser subsided, and Clara's limp body sank to the bed.

140

Gorgas ventured forward to wipe the vomit off Clara's face, but just as his hand reached out, the body shot up again, and he felt the warm liquid hit his cheek. Guiteras had backed off into a corner and stood there, the back of his hand pressed against his nostrils. His usually well-controlled face had lost its professional mask. Horror and pity twisted it instead as though he had unexpectedly bitten into a very, very sour orange.

This time there was no stopping the volcanic flow that poured from inside. The body jerked up and down as though it was being manipulated like a puppet on strings. The dark red vomit sprayed everything, sheets, blankets, pillow. It plopped on the floor and trickled slowly down the walls.

Clara was tearing at her throat, choking and gasping, as her body was heaved and tossed by the explosive powers bursting from within. Her terrified blue eyes stared fixedly at Gorgas, an undefinable stricken stare. And then there was one last explosive sucking heave that died away in a low sigh, and the body collapsed on the bed. Slight quivers and tremors continued to ripple through the frame, but the flow from the open mouth had diminished to a thin red stream. Clara's eyes, still open, stared at the ceiling.

"A martyr to science," whispered Dr. Guiteras, brushing his cheeks as he walked from the room with Dr. Gorgas.

Gorgas said nothing. His cheeks glistened and his beard quivered convulsively.

At his office Dr. Gorgas sat down at his desk. He sat, shading his eyes with his hand. For a long time he sat. Then he picked up his phone, and with muffled voice spoke into it.

"A wire please to Mrs. Robert Maass, East Orange, New Jersey. It should read—"his voice broke. He struggled for control, then went on, 'Miss Maass died twenty-fourth, six-thirty.' Sign it Gorgas.

The telegram was delivered first, not to Clara's mother, but to her sister Sophie, as she stepped off the steamer from New York which dropped anchor in Havana Bay the next day. With trembling fingers Sophie ripped open the envelope and read the message. Then she crumpled silently to the pavement.

As for Dr. Gorgas, he went home to his wife. With voice breaking with both sorrow and anger he declared, "Marie, I finally am convinced that the mosquito is the carrier, and, Marie," his voice, though tremulous with grief, vibrated also with determination, "I am going to rid Havana of mosquitoes." ■

16

Yellow Jack Driven Out

Gorgas did rid Havana of mosquitoes, as impossible as that had seemed to be. He threw himself into the crusade he had launched months earlier at Wood's coaxing. With determination, patience, gentleness, courtesy, and a fastidious attention to detail, within a few months Gorgas won. When General Wood, May 20, 1902, handed over the government to Tomas Palma, the first president of the Republic of Cuba, the island was as free of the tyranny of yellow fever as of the tyranny of Spain. Only once in 1905 did it flare up, to be quickly put out by Gorgas's methods. From that day to this, yellow fever has not taken toll of lives.

From Cuba, Gorgas moved on to Panama. He long had dreamed of a canal being dug there, but knew that tropical fevers prevented this venture. By 1906 Gorgas had freed Panama of yellow fever.

Rio de Janeiro and Vera Cruz were next. Guayaquil, Ecuador, reported its last case in 1919.

July 3, 1920, Gorgas died while in England. That same year yellow fever epidemics broke out in Peru, Brazil, Honduras, Salvador, Mexico, Nicaragua, and Guatemala. Apprehensive medical men began to suspect that yellow fever was not going to be as easily overcome as they had hoped. The puzzle Clara had referred to was proving to be much more difficult to put together than any had ever dreamed.

Many years of diligent research followed. Later research uncovered the fact that not only the Aedes aegypti but 20 species of mosquitoes carried yellow fever. Nor was it necessary for these mosquitoes to bite infected human beings, for in Africa, researches discovered, even monkeys could have yellow fever. The identification of jungle yellow fever brought new problems.

After a long time scientists tracked down what caused yellow fever, a filterable virus, invisible under even the most powerful lens of a microscope. It has been described as "a spherical particle measuring from one to two millions of an inch in diameter, and, like the living cell nucleus, largely made up of nucleic acid and proteins."

The search for a safe serum for immunization was even more frustrating and costly. One serum that immunized against yellow fever, in some cases, produced encephalitis and had to be abandoned. Another vaccine containing human serum produced hepatitis. This vaccine also was discarded. The unwritten law in vaccine-making is that you must not create an actual danger to head off a potential one.

The search went on for years. The Rockefeller Foundation spent more than $12 million from 1916 to 1949 fighting yellow fever, more than they spent on any other specific disease. By World War II a safe vaccine, at least for all over 10 years of age, had been developed. The vaccine was grown in the eggs of chickens. So successful was this vaccine that during the entire war not one American soldier contracted yellow fever.

But achievement has been at an inestimable cost. The roster of brilliant scientists who gave their lives as they worked in the laboratories include names like Lazear, Myers, Cross, Stokes,

144

Noguchi, and Young. Added to these are countless volunteers. But the only woman and the only nurse whose name appears on that roster is that of Clara Louise Maass. By earning a place there, the poor little mother's helper from East Orange, N.J., attained for her life the lasting significance for which she had longed. ■

BOTTOM: Clara Maass Hospital today; moved to Belleview N.Y. in 1957; MIDDLE LEFT: Clara Maass grave marker, Fairmount Cemetery, New Jersey; MIDDLE LEFT: Albin Oberg (left) and Harold Widman, of Clara Maass Memorial Hospital administration, study artist, Paul Calle's original sketches of Clara Maass commemorative stamp; TOP LEFT: First day commemorative stamp ceremony at Clara Maass Hospital; TOP RIGHT: Clara Maass stamp issued by the U.S. Postal Department.

17

In Dying She Lives

Sophie Maass lingered in Havana long enough to see sister Clara buried in a lead coffin in Havana's Colon Cemetery. Tropical climate demanded that burial be within 24 hours. Then Sophie went back to Clara's room, gathered up her sister's belongings, and took a ship back to New Jersey.

The New York Journal ran Clara's story on the front page of its edition of Monday, Aug. 26, complete with pictures. The editor of the New York Times wrote about Clara's death (misspelling her name):

> The ethics of the Cuban experiments would seem to depend a good deal upon the motive actuating the victims. In the case of Miss Maas, the young nurse who died on Saturday, it would seem to have been the very highest which could inspire a self-sacrificing woman to put her life in peril. She not only was willing to incur the risk of infection if thereby she might assist in establishing a scientific hypothesis of first importance in the etiology of yellow fever, but she

desired to make herself immune, to the end that her usefulness in her chosen vocation might be increased and her opportunities of service to those suffering from the disease enlarged beyond what would be possible in one liable to contract the disease. No soldier in the late war placed his life in peril for better reasons than those which prompted this faithful nurse to risk hers. Facing death on the battlefield does not call for the highest kind of courage. Thousands who would have rushed up San Juan Hill with a shout would turn pale at the thought of facing less imminent danger in the quiet of the clinic, as the subjects of an experiment like that of a bite from an infected insect that might or might not, be capable of imparting the disease she is supposed to carry.

The annals of medicine are full of the records of the noblest and most disinterested self-sacrifice for the sake of truth. Unmarked and forgotten graves are filled by those who have joined the noble army of martyrs and left behind as their legacy to humanity facts to assist in formulating the generalizations of medical science.

As publicity grew, the Army recognized the service she had performed. They ordered her lead casket dug up and sent to New Jersey, where it was placed, with military honors, in Fairmount Cemetery, within easy walking distance from her mother's home on Main Street. A small army stone marked the place. In 1904 the army granted Clara's mother a pension of $12 a month in recognition of her daughter's service which they considered "of a military character at the time of her death."

The Committee on Pensions declared that her case "had much more effect in the city of Havana in convincing the physicians and people generally that yellow fever was conveyed by the mosquito than did the work of the army board. In this way the assistance and cooperation of the people in our mosquito work was obtained. From this point of view the death of Miss Maass greatly contributed to establishing the fact that yellow fever was conveyed by mosquitoes."

At Newark German Hospital brief acknowledgment was made that Clara had been one of its first and finest nurses. And then the hospital got on with their job of continuing to care for the sick and balance their budget, which much of the time seemed to

148

teeter on the edge of bankruptcy. After all, was not responding to duty a daily way of life?

Finally in 1910 the Alumnae Association decided they should do something to perpetuate the memory of Clara. After much discussion they decided to endow a room in her memory which could be used for alumnae members or nurses who became ill. The room was dedicated in November 1912. At that time the graduate nurses also unveiled a crayon portrait of Clara which they hung over the fireplace in the living room of the nurses' quarters.Dr. Edward Staehlin, in his dedicatory address, said:

> . . . We admire the hero who falls in battle, but he is urged on amid countless numbers to the tune of martial music to fight the cause of the oppressor's wrong, hopeful ever of being spared. We admire in any walk of life the one who succumbs to duty's call, yet the outcome here is usually unlooked for and rarely anticipated. They are hallowed endings, but not to be compared with the ending of the one who solitary and alone avows a cause whose issue brings self-destruction for the benefit of all posterity. So toil the workmen who repair the world!

Another early recognition of Clara's contribution to science came when, in 1916, W. B. Saunders Company of Philadelphia published Minnie Goodnow's textbook for nurses, Nursing History. In the section referring to the posts nurses filled in the Spanish American War Miss Goodnow wrote of Clara Maass:

> Special mention should be made of Clara Maass, of New Jersey, a graduate nurse who, while on active duty helped with research. Among others, she allowed herself to be bitten by mosquitoes carrying yellow fever, and died as the result of her devotion to science. Her name is worthy to stand with that of Walter Reed.

The years passed. The nursing school at the German Hospital grew. The number of patients increased. During World War I the name "German" was dropped, and the hospital became simply "Newark Memorial Hospital."

In the 1920s a maternity wing was added. In 1923 a new superintendent of nursing arrived, Miss Leopoldine Guinther, a graduate of the Philadelphia General Hospital School of Nursing. Noticing Clara's picture and the room bearing her name, Miss Guinther repeatedly asked who Clara Maass was. "A former chief nurse" was the only answer she received.

Feb. 20, 1927, Miss Guinther sat reading the Newark Evening News. She glanced at the "25 Years Ago Today" column. A name caught her eye. Clara Maass. "The body of Clara L. Maass," the column noted, "who died of yellow fever in Cuba, has been shipped to Newark and there buried with military honors."

Military honors! Miss Guinther determined to learn more. She located Clara's mother, past 80, living in a home for the aged. She uncovered Clara's grave, overgrown with weeds. She made a trip to Cuba, but all it yielded was the suggestion that she try to locate government documents telling about the experiments. She did. Some were in Spanish. She copied them and made another trip to Cuba to get them translated. By now she was so captivated by Clara's story that she vowed to keep Clara's memory alive.

She began by having Dr. Staehlin's dedicatory words copied on parchment, framed, and placed in the living room for nurses.

She begged money from everyone she knew to erect in 1930 a polished pink Milford granite headstone over Clara's grave. On the headstone Miss Guinther placed a bronze tablet with a likeness of Clara and a paragraph about her life. At the bottom she had engraved: "Greater love hath no man than this."

And then Miss Guinther resigned from the hospital, and for a while Clara was almost forgotten.

Down in Havana, Cuba, however, Dr. Antonio Diaz Albertini remembered. Sept. 28, 1936, he unveiled a Clara Maass plaque in the Las Animas Hospital.

Clara's sister, Emma, dedicated, in Clara's memory, a beautiful stained-glass window of Christ in Gethsemane in Mountain View Methodist Church in 1941.

But at the hospital little more was done to remember Clara until the Lutheran churches took over the hospital and Rev. Arthur Herbert became involved.

The Lutheran take-over came about because the hospital

never had been able to recover from the blow the depression dealt it. The staff had done all they could to save money. They rolled their own bandages and sterlized their own instruments. They managed with four bed pans for 25 patients. The nurses ran up and down the stairs because the creaky old elevator cost two cents every time it moved. The nurses painted beds. They toted the one adjustable spring bed they had from floor to floor. But the hospital was still reeling by 1944. When it seemed inevitable that it would close, the staff took up a collection. They presented $8,100 to the directors.

But it was clear that action had to be taken. In December Dr. Robert Jonitz was asked by the administration to approach Rev. Arthur Herbert of Holy Trinity Lutheran Church, Orange, to inquire if the Lutheran churches would like to take on the support of a hospital.

Pastor Herbert brought the matter before his church council. The council met with hospital representatives on Dec. 21 at the Downtown Club in Newark.

A larger group of Lutheran pastors and lay persons met with hospital doctors and directors at Dr. Crecca's home on Feb. 1. May 22, 1945, Newark Memorial Hospital became Lutheran Memorial Hospital.

The move was significant for keeping the memory of Clara Maass alive.

Pastor Herbert threw himself into the work of the hospital. As he dug around in the records, he came upon the story of Clara. Deeply moved by her sacrifice, he featured her on the 1949 Christmas seal of the hospital. Then, why stop with one stamp? he asked. Why not try to get a U. S. stamp issued?

But getting approval for a U. S. stamp to commemorate the memory of a person is not easy. At least 50 years must pass, the Postmaster General told Pastor Herbert.

Pastor Herbert determined to find other ways to keep alive the memory of the "heroine of the tropics," as he referred to Clara.

In 1949 Time magazine ran an article on yellow fever. "You forgot to mention Clara Maass," Pastor Herbert wrote the Time

151

editors, relating her story. They published his letter and Clara's picture.

Astonishing results followed. The American Weekly and nearly a score of smaller magazines featured articles on Clara.

Dr. Walter Maier referred to her on Memorial Day on "The Lutheran Hour" programs that were broadcast over 1,100 stations in 50 countries and in 20 languages.

E. I. du Pont de Nemours and Co. took note and ran radio and television versions of "No Greater Love" on its Cavalcade of America.

Still pastor Herbert was not satisfied. In 1949 the Lutheran Memorial Hospital established two $400 Clara Maass scholarships for Cuban girls who wanted to study nursing at the Newark Hospital.

Upsala College named one of their new dormitories "Clara Maass Hall' in 1950. Las Animas Hospital in Havana dedicated a pavilion in her honor. Holy Trinity Lutheran Church of Havana started a new college, declaring they would call it Colegio Clara Maass. On Aug. 24, 1951, Cuba issued a postage stamp bearing Clara's picture and a drawing of both the old German Hospital and Las Animas Hospital.

But the most permanent recognition came on June 19, 1952. The Lutheran Memorial Hospital decided Clara should be remembered with more than just a portrait and a room. It relinquished its old name and took Clara's.

As the years moved on, Clara Maass Memorial Hospital began to show signs of age. The neighborhood too around the hospital deteriorated. Nursing classes grew smaller and smaller because parents hesitated to let their daughters live in the area.

Twenty-eight-year-old Albin H. Oberg, who had become executive director, studied and pondered the situation. Then, Julius A. Rippel, a son of one of the original founders of the German Hospital, gave the hospital a gift of $1 million toward building a new hospital at a more favorable location. Additional loans and pledges were needed. Months of negotiations followed. But, as the new Clara Maass Memorial Hospital rose slowly in 1955 and 1956, Clara's picture and story were carried in 800 magazines, and the Public

Service Advertising Council featured her in a 1956 advertisement for United States Savings Bonds.

The day the patients were to be transferred from the old hospital to the new, Mrs. Irene Jordan, admitting clerk, arrived at the new hospital to find her first patient waiting for her. Mrs. Elizina Nunes and her husband, Manuel, were seated on the curb. A little over an hour after the transfer of all the patients had been completed in the afternoon, Mrs. Nunes gave birth to a little girl. The Nunes named her Clara Maass. Clara now had a living memorial.

The hospital grew and grew, adding wings and additional stories, nurses' quarters, and 30 doctors' offices. By the spring of 1966, 419 beds were ready to receive patients.

Ground for a Continuing Care Center was broken in 1969. By 1971 the number of beds had increased to 570.

One goal remained to be accomplished. Though Pastor Herbert had worked tirelessly to get a U.S. stamp in Clara's honor, he never had succeeded. But after he died, Harold Widman, the hospital's vice-president for public relations and James Clements, publisher, and Richard F. Newcomb, editor of RN Magazine, with the assistance of Howard B. Hurley, the magazine's specialist in nursing philately, took up the cause. Couldn't Clara be remembered on her 100th birthday?

At the invitation of Widman and Hurley, Dr. Fernando Lopez Fernandez of Chicago, a Cuban physician, who had been instrumental in seeing Cuba's Clara Maass stamp issued in 1951, accepted the honorary chairmanship of the committee.

For six years the committee worked. Eventually people from nearly every state in the nation were involved. After receiving thousands of letters and petitions generated by RN's nationwide subscriber audience, plus endorsements solicited by the committee from virtually every leader in the health professions and many government officials, Postmaster General Benjamin F. Bailer wrote the hospital trustees and the staff of RN Magazine:

> In the very near future, we will be announcing the subjects of several commemorative stamps to be issued in 1976 and, because of your

previous interest, I wanted you to know in advance that one of the issuances will honor Clara Maass, the heroic nurse who gave her life in yellow fever research.

When the official Postal Service announcement was released, it stated, in part: "Numerous requests for commemorative stamps were submitted for approval and issue during the Nation's Bicentennial year. The Clara Maass stamp was one of only seven single commemorative stamps selected for issue during 1976."

The Clara Maass Memorial Hospital's and RN Magazine's goal of honoring Clara Maass, and through her, all American nurses, had been accomplished.

Connecticut artist Paul Calle was selected to design the stamp. Calle noted that his daughter, Claudia, graduated in June 1976 from Columbia University's Presbyterian Hospital on the 100th anniversary of Clara's birth. And Claudia became a nurse.

Calle's design for the stamp was unveiled Sunday, June 6, in dramatic ceremonies viewed by a vast audience at the American Nurses Association Convention in Atlantic City. At the same time, Clara Maass joined 14 other nursing pioneers in the newly established Nursing Hall of Fame.

Sunday, June 27, was designated as Clara Maass Sunday in the Belleville, N.J., area. An order-of-service bulletin was prepared, with a picture of the stained glass window in Mountain View Methodist Church dedicated to Miss Maass by her younger sister, Emma. This bulletin was used by more than 100 churches in the area on that Sunday.

The State Senate and the Assembly adopted resolutions commemorating Clara's 100th birthday and had them read into the Congressional Records, noting her dates of service as an Army nurse: 1 October 1898 to 5 February 1899 and 20 November 1899 to 7 May 1900. June 28 was proclaimed Clara Maass day in Belleville and Nutley. Graveside ceremonies at Newark's Fairmount Cemetery were held.

August 18, 1976, the Clara Maass commemorative stamp was issued at the Clara Maass Memorial Hospital. Military and Civilian leaders of the nursing profession, high-ranking postal officials, state and local dignitaries all thronged to the hospital. Clara Maass Nunes, now 19, attended and was recognized at the stamp's First Day of Issue ceremonies. Plaques were unveiled, Clara Maasss' buttons and a folder were distributed. A 600-lb. birthday cake served 2,500 people. The cake, designed, baked, and donated by Francis Cake Specialties of Belleville, featured a three-dimensional portrait of Clara in full colors. Two hundred pounds of butter cream were needed to ice the cake.

In October guests at the Clara Maass Centennial Ball declared that proceeds from the ball should go for the Cancer Treatment Center at the hospital to be opened a short while later.

Helene Fuld Health Trust technicians taped the entire Centennial event at the hospital to show to 168 nursing schools throughout the country.

If she had been present, Clara would have been the most astonished of all. She would have protested that she had done only what Christ calls all of us to do: to love our neighbor as ourselves, and not to hold our lives as dear to ourselves. But surely at the same time Clara would have been cheered to note that people esteem service to others and do not forget lives poured out in loving sacrifice. It was of such as Clara that Jesus Christ, the most selfless of all servants of the sick and suffering, declared: "There is no greater love!" ■

"Greater love hath no man than this."

Bibliography

Brown, Charles H. The Correspondents' War. New York: Charles Scribner's Sons, 1967.

Bullough, Vern L. and Bonnie. The Emergence of Modern Nursing. London: The Macmillan Co., 1969.

Chidsey, Donald Barr. The Spanish-American War. New York: Crown Publishers, Inc., 1971.

Cosmos, Graham A. An Army for Empire: The U. S. in the Spanish-American War. Columbia, Missouri: University of Missouri Press, 1971.

Cunningham, John T. Clara Maass: A Nurse, a Hospital, a Spirit. Belleville, N. J.: Clara Maass Hospital, 1976.

Dietz, Lena Dixon and Lehozky, Aurelia R. History and Modern Nursing. Philadelphia: F. A. Davis Co., 1967.

Dock, Lavinia L. A History of Nursing. New York and London: G. P. Putnam's Sons, 1912.

Dolan, Jospehine A. Goodnow's History of Nursing. Philadelphia: W. B. Saunders Company, 1963.

Eberle, Irmengarde. Nurse! New York: Thomas Y. Crowell Co., 1945.

Epler, Percy H. The Life of Clara Barton. New York: The Macmillan Co., 1937.

Finlay, Carlos E. Carlos Finlay and Yellow Fever. New York: Oxford University Press, 1940.

Friedel, Frank. The Splendid Little War. Boston: Little, Brown and Company, 1958.

Gatewood, Willard B., Jr. Smoked Yankee and the Struggle for Empire. Urbana, Chicago, and Illinois: University of Illinois Press, 1971.

Gibson, John M. Physician to the World. Durham, N. C.: Duke University Press, 1950.

Goodnow, Minnie. Nursing History in Brief. Philadelphia: W. B. Saunders Company, 1950.

——Nursing History. Philadelphia: W. B. Saunders Company, 1960.

Gorgas, Marie D. and Hendrick, Burton J. William Crawford Gorgas, His Life and Work. Garden City: Garden City Publishing Co., 1924.

Hagedorn, Hermann. Leonard Wood. New York and London: Harper and Bros., 1931.

Hume, Ruth Fox. Great Women of Medicine. New York: Random House, 1964.

Jamieson, Elizabeth M. and Sewall, Mary F. Trends in Nursing History. Philadelphia: W. B. Saunders Company, 1949.

Keating, J. M., A History of The Yellow Fever: The Yellow Fever Epidemic of 1878, in Memphis, Tennessee. Memphis: The Howard Association, 1879.

Kelly, H. A. Walter Reed and Yellow Fever. New York: Doubleday, 2d ed., 1906.

Kennan, George, Campaigning in Cuba. Port Washington, N. Y.: Kennikat Press, reissued 1971.

Lampson, Robin. Death Loses a Pair of Wings. New York: Charles Scribner's Sons, 1939.

Lawson, Don. The United States in the Spanish-American War. New York: Abelard-Schuman, 1976.

Lightfoot, Keith. The Philippines. New York, Washington: Praeger Publishers, 1973.

Marks, Geoffrey and Beatty, William K. Women in White. New York: Charles Scribner's Sons, 1972.

Miller, Richard H., ed. American Imperialism in 1898. New York: John Wiley and Sons, Inc., 1970.

Post, Charles Johnson. The Little War of Private Post. Boston: Little, Brown and Co., 1960.

Roberts, Mary M. American Nursing, History and Interpretation. New York: The Macmillan Company, 1954.

Robinson, Victor. White Caps. Philadelphia and New York: J. B. Lippincott Company, 1946.

Shippen, Katherine B. Men of Medicine. New York: The Viking Press, 1957.

Stanley, Peter W. A Nation in the Making, The Philippines and the U. S., 1899—1921. Cambridge, Mass.: Harvard University Press, 1974.

Stewart, Isabel M. and Austin, Anne L. A History of Nursing. New York: G. P. Putnam's Sons, 1962.

Thomas, Hugh. Cuba, the Pursuit of Freedom. New York: Harper & Row, 1971.

Williams, Blanche Colton. Clara Barton: Daughter of Destiny. Philadelphia: J. B. Lippincott Co., 1941.

Williams, Greer. The Plague Killers. New York: Charles Scribner's Sons. 1969.

Williams, Beryl and Epstein, Samuel. <u>William Crawford Gorgas.</u> New York: Julian Messner, Inc., 1961.

Articles, Pamphlets, and Documents

Agramonte A. "The Inside Story of a Great Medical Discovery." <u>Scientific Monthly</u> (Dec. 1915), pp. 209—237.

<u>The American Weekly.</u> (May 8, 1949.)

"Clara Louise Maass." <u>The American Journal of Nursing.</u> (June 1950), 50:343.

"Clara Maass." <u>RN Magazine</u> (Feb. 1973).

Cuba, Military Governor, Leonard Wood. Civil Report, 1899-1900. Vol. IV, 1900. Washington: Government Printing Office.

Cuba, Military Governor, Leonard Wood. Civil Report, 1900—1901. Vol. IV, 1901. Washington: Government Printing Office.

<u>The East Orange Record,</u> East Orange, N. J. Six articles on Clara Maass, spring of 1945.

Guinter, Leopoldine, "A Nurse among the Heroes of the Yellow Fever Conquest." <u>The American Journal of Nursing.</u> Vol. XXXII. No. 2. Feb. 1932.

Hughes, Robert L. <u>The Great Destroyers.</u> Health Officer, Calhoun County, Anniston, Ala., 1915. Containing verbatim the testimony of Dr. Gorgas.

Hurley, Howard B. "Clara Maass—A Nurse, a Spirit, a Stamp." <u>Proceedings Sixty-Third Annual Meeting, New Jersey Mosquito Control Assn.,</u> Inc. (March 10—12, 1976). Cherry Hill, N.J.

"Maass Memo." Clara Maass Memorial Hospital Belleville, N. J. (1976)

Moore, John Bassett. "Gorgas, Redeemer of the Tropics," <u>American Review of Reviews,</u> LXV, 188—194 (Feb. 1922).

Research notes prepared for Dr. Josiah C. Trent (April 1945) from Army Medical Dept.

"<u>RN Magazine</u> Represented at Stamp Unveiling." <u>RN Magazine</u> (Aug. 1976).

"RN Notes and Quotes." <u>RN Magazine</u> (April 1974).

U. S. Senate. Yellow Fever: <u>A Compilation of Various Publications: Results of the Work of Maj. Walter Reed, Medical Corps, United States Army, and the Yellow Fever Commission,</u> U. S. Senate Document, No. 822. 61st Congress, 3d Session. Washington D.C.: Government Printing Office, 1911.

"U.S. Stamp to Honor Clara Maass." <u>RN Magazine</u> (Sept. 1975 and June 1976).

U. S. War Department. Annual Report, 1900—1901. Report of the Lieutenant-General Commanding the Army, 7 volumes. 56th Congress, House of Representatives. Washington D. C.: Government Printing Office, 1901.

Archives and other sources include a copy of a personal letter from Sophie Maass Kapps and a copy of Clara Maass' medical record.